A theatrical feud that erupted into mob violence is described in this lively account of the great riot that occurred in Astor Place, New York City, on the night of May 10, 1849. At the fashionable Astor Place Opera House the noted British tragedian, William Macready, was playing *Macbeth*. Farther downtown, at the Broadway Theatre, his equally famous American rival, Edwin Forrest, was appearing in *The Gladiator*. While Forrest was being cheered to the echo by true blue Americans, other true blue Americans, incited by local newspapers, were heaving eggs at the unfortunate Macready; and outside the Opera House a hundred police and militiamen were trying to repel the onslaught of a gang of toughs known as the Bowery B'hoys. Brickbats and musket balls flew through the air as some ten thousand spectators watched the fray, and when the smoke of battle cleared thirty-one killed and a hundred and fifty wounded were carted away.

Thus was the honor of America, represented by "Ned" Forrest, the native son, defended against the pretensions of the British invader and his supporters among New York's social elite — the "codfish aristocracy." The whole tragi-comic episode, with its background and aftermath, is dramatically presented in this entertaining story, which incidentally throws a vivid light on the formation of public opinion in nineteenth-century America.

*Astor
*Place
Riot

RICHARD MOODY

*   *   *   *

the

* Astor

* Place

* Riot

*   *   *

INDIANA UNIVERSITY PRESS

BLOOMINGTON   1958

FOR

Carol, Pam, and Craig

Contents

Illustrations

*Astor
*Place
Riot

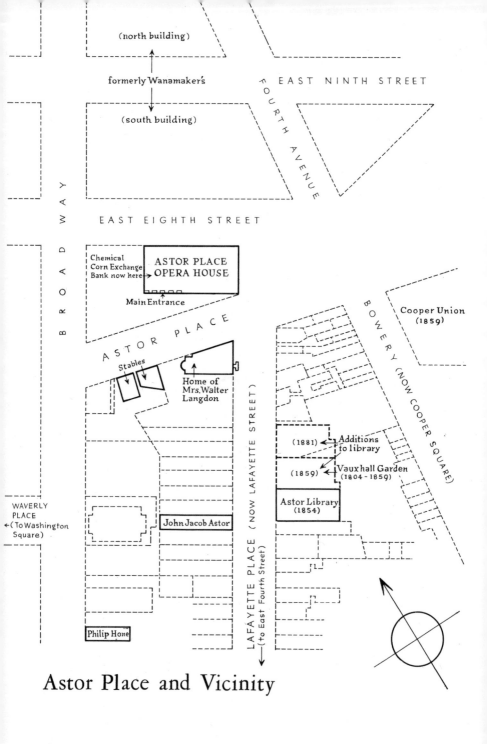

Astor Place and Vicinity

As It Happened

CHAPTER ONE

In July, 1956, the deserted north building of what had been Wanamaker's Department Store, in lower Manhattan between East Eighth Street and East Tenth, was gutted by a five-alarm fire that lasted for two days. If among the hundreds of observers there was a historian of local affairs, he might have thought back somewhat more than a century to the night of the Astor Place Theatre riot. On that night, at about ten o'clock, he would have been obliged to cross East Eighth Street between two cordons of police, one extending across the east end of the block (at the corner now occupied by the Chemical Corn Exchange

Bank) and the other across the Broadway end. Then as now, Astor Place, Lafayette Place (now Lafayette Street), and East Eighth Street converge on a sizable square. On the night of the riot, Thursday, May 10, 1849, this area was occupied by a mob of enraged citizens battering one another in what appeared to be a gigantic free-for-all. An imposing, classically façaded edifice was being defended by a hundred or so ill-disposed and carelessly uniformed militiamen against the disorganized attack of some ten thousand rioters who were waving clubs and throwing paving stones, bricks, and street debris.

The building in question was the fashionable Astor Place Opera House, or Theatre—the terms were used interchangeably. It occupied a small, almost triangular plot bounded on the north by East Eighth Street, on the south by Astor Place, on the west by Broadway, and on the east by what was then known as the Bowery. In the neighborhood, as the fatalities increased, a scattering of "morgues" were improvised to house the bodies of those who were killed in the riot. This event had climaxed a long-standing feud between two actors, William C. Macready and Edwin Forrest, one a "silk-stockinged" Englishman and the other a "true-blue" son of America.

Ignorant as the twentieth-century New Yorker may be of the riot and of its prelude and aftermath, his predecessors in the mid-nineteenth century were fully aware that trouble was brewing at the Opera House. A large share of the crowd that night was made up of "innocent bystanders" just passing by to enjoy the excitement. A fury of rebellious yells and a colorful tirade of abusive language were to be expected. Perhaps a few stones would be thrown and a few obstreperous individuals clubbed—a token demonstration by the forces of law and order—but that was all that the crowd anticipated.

The city officials sensed that there was more in the wind. At eleven o'clock on the morning of May 10, 1849, Caleb S. Woodhull, Mayor of the city and county of New York, being informed, as he said, "that there was likely to be a disturbance at the theatre in Astor Place," called a conference in his office. The conferees were Recorder Tallmadge, Sheriff Westervelt, Chief of Police Matsell, Major General Sandford, commanding the military forces of the county, and Messrs. Niblo and Hackett, proprietors of the theatre. Woodhull preferred to cancel the performance, close the theatre, and be done with the problem; but Niblo and Hackett, with a full house assured and a company engaged, were disinclined to leave the theatre dark. As Niblo said, "They had put out their bills and they proposed to play." If there were a disturbance in prospect, it was the Mayor's duty to see that order was maintained. Woodhull weakly agreed to accept this responsibility and proceeded to canvass his advisors on the possible courses of action.

Chief of Police Matsell, the most pessimistic of the group, looked for a serious disorder and was certain that his civil forces would be unequal to the demands. General Sandford remarked "that it was not for him to say whether or not the militia should be ordered out; it was his business to obey the orders." Forced to a decision, Woodhull prepared a general order as to the number of militiamen to be called out and instructed Matsell and Sandford "to take such measures, and act as the occasion required."

While this conclave for law and order met, the "Bowery B'hoys" were busy around town distributing notices and posting placards encouraging any and all to turn up for the

evening's fun at the "English Aristocratic Opera House."
The B'hoys, many of them members of the Order of United
Americans (forerunner of the Know-Nothing Party) were
a miscellaneous congregation of hoodlums and hotheads
from the Bowery district. They were led by E. Z. C. Judson,
an adventurer and rabble-rouser who was better known as
"Ned Buntline."

At twenty minutes to six, when Macready arrived at the
theatre, the house was filling rapidly. With money pouring
into the box office so freely, Niblo and Hackett had no scru-
ples about selling more tickets than there were seats, maintaining that peace was not their problem. Macready was
equally unworried, if his diary speaks truthfully, but he may
have been whistling in the dark.

I went gaily, I may say, to the theatre, and on my way, looking
down Astor Place, saw one of the Harlem cars on the railroad
stop, discharge a full load of policemen; there seemed to be others
at the doors of the theatre. I observed to myself: "This is good
precaution." I went to my dressing room, and proceeded with the
evening's business. The hairdresser was very late, and my equa-
nimity was disturbed. I was ruffled and nervous, from fear of
being late, but soon composed myself.

He could hear the crowd above and the applause that
greeted the entrance of Mr. Clarke, an American and the
Macduff for the evening. "I was called, and at my cue, went
with full assurance, confidence and cheerfulness. My reception was very enthusiastic, but I soon discovered there was
opposition." Macready was prepared; his haughty stare
would subdue the scoundrels. "Looking at the wretched
creatures in the parquet who shook their fists violently at
me, and called out to me in savage fury, I laughed at them,
pointing them out with my truncheon to the police." A

blackboard had been placed against the proscenium with a scribbled message: "The friends of order will remain silent." As Macready says, "This, too, had some effect in making the rioters more conspicuous."

The first three scenes went rapidly but were unheard above the commotion. "At the end of the fourth," Macready reports, "one of the officers gave a signal, the police rushed in at the two sides of the parquet, closed in upon the scoundrels occupying the centre seats, furiously vociferating and gesticulating, and seemed to lift or bundle them in a body out of the centre of the house, amid the cheers of the audience." Macready was more occupied with these troubles than with those of Macbeth. "I was in the act of making my exit with Lady Macbeth, and stopped to witness this clever manoeuvre, which like a *coup de main,* swept the place clear at once."

But Macready's exit, rather than marking the end of the action, signalled the beginning of the major event of the evening, the storming of the theatre. As if by some prearranged cue, the arrest of the rioters inside the theatre was the call to arms for those outside. The shelter of the wings seems to have provided little safety, as Macready reports the opening of the bombardment.

Stones were hurled against the windows in Eighth Street, smashing many; the work of destruction became then more systematic; the volleys of stones flew without intermission, battering and smashing all before them. As I was going to my raised seat in the banquet scene, Mr. Povey came up to me, and, in an undertone, and much frightened, urged me to cut out some part of the play and bring it to a close. I turned round upon him very sharply, and said that I had consented to do this thing to place myself here, and, whatever the consequence, I must go through with it—it must be done; that I would not cut out. The audience had paid for so much, and the law compelled me to give it. They would have cause for riot, if all were not properly done. I was angry, and I spoke very sharply to the above effect.

Macready, never timid about reporting his bravery, refused to recognize that a riot was under way. Even after discovering that his dressing room was being flooded—a stone had broken some of the pipes—he went on stage for the fourth act.

His diary describes the action eloquently:

Louder and more fierce waxed the furious noises against the building, for whenever a missile did effectual mischief in its discharge, it was hailed with shouts outside. Stones came in through the windows, and one struck the chandelier. The audience removed for protection behind the walls. The house was considerably thinned, gaps of unoccupied seats appearing in the audience part. The fifth act was heard, and in the very spirit of resistance I flung my whole soul into every word I uttered, acting my very best, and exciting the audience to a sympathy even with the glowing words of fiction, while these dreadful deeds of real crime and outrage were roaring at intervals in our ears, and rising to madness all around us. The death of Macbeth was loudly cheered, and, on being lifted up and told that I was called, I went on, and, with action earnestly and most emphatically expressive of my sympathy with them and my feelings of gratefulness to them, I quitted the New York stage amid the acclamations of those before me.

When Macready was ready to leave the theatre, "the consternation on the faces of some, fear, anxiety and distress on those of others," who had come to his dressing room, and the volleys of musketry he could now hear, informed him of the "degree of danger" he now faced. The assault on the theatre building was a provisional substitute for a direct attack on his person. Macready sensed this, and although he favored "meeting the worst with dignity," his friends forced a disguise on him, "the drab surtout of the performer of Malcolm and Mr. Sefton's cap." Thus equipped he headed with his protectors for the stage door. Here they were stopped. Macready again reports what happened:

Not being allowed to pass, we crossed the stage, descended into the orchestra, got over into the parquet, and passing into the centre passage, went along with the thin stream of audience moving out. We went right on, down the flight of stairs, and out of the door into Eighth Street. All was clear in front—kept so by two cordons or lines of police at either end of the building, stretched right across. We passed the line near Broadway and went on threading the excited crowd, twice or three times muttering in Emmett's ear, "You are walking too fast." We crossed Broadway still through a scattered crowd, and walked along Clinton Place till we passed the street leading down to the New York Hotel. I then said: "Are you going to your own house," "Yes." We reached it, and having opened the door with a latch-key, closing it after us, he said: "You are safe here; no one will know anything about you; you shall have a bed in ten minutes or a quarter of an hour, and you may depend on all in this house."

Macready holed in here for the next three hours and then was hustled off to New Rochelle. In the morning he took the train for Boston and after twelve days in seclusion boarded the *Hibernia* for the journey back to England.

If the police had passed Macready through the stage door into Astor Place, or if he had turned east when he stepped into Eighth Street, he would at least have observed the bloody turmoil that had been provoked. As it was, he saw only the indignities inside the theatre and nothing of the fatal massacre outside.

The curtain had gone up on the demonstration in front of the theatre two hours before the *Macbeth* witches began their incantations, and it was not finally rung down until after the trial of the rioters, four months later. By the late afternoon of this bloody Thursday, few inhabitants of New York were unaware of the big doings at the Opera House. Many of them were already at the scene. The anti-Macready forces had bought up what tickets they could earlier in the day and were on hand to take their places when the doors opened. All paths led to Astor Place. "Thousands of men were seen walking rapidly up Broadway"; some came along Eighth Street, some on the Harlem cars, and still more from the Bowery. During the afternoon the windows of the theatre had been carefully barricaded with inch-and-a-half boards, and by curtain time almost the entire city police force had been stationed in and around the theatre. When the house had been declared full, every entrance was plugged up with a police guard to push back the rowdies who were intent on getting in without tickets. There was at the beginning, however, no concerted attempt to storm the theatre; nor did the anti-Macready forces seem to have any prearranged battle plan.

When the curtain went up inside, the crowd outside began to test its strength. The partisans' abusive howls and yells soon encouraged the hesitant bystanders to join in. In a few minutes, cries of "Down with Macready!" "Burn the damned den of the Aristocracy!" were exploding against the building with the force of a thousand angry voices. But the mounting resentment against the English actor was not to be satisfied by shouts. Someone (identity unknown) threw the first stone, and the thrilling crash of glass, accompanied by the victorious cheers of the mob, created the moment for the opening of a full barrage. The attackers discovered a stock pile of ammunition immediately available, a pile of paving stones that had been dug out for the construction of a sewer. The police were helpless. Some managed to get inside the building, but most of them had to pull away from it and venture into the street in order to escape the falling rocks. Thus they found themselves in the awkward, if temporarily more comfortable, position of having the enemy both in front and behind, with the stones sailing overhead. Benjamin P. Fairchild, Captain of the Eighth Ward Police, reported his view of this early action:

I was directed by the Chief to report to him if at any time I thought it was necessary to send for the military, to sustain our position, but not to do so if there was a possibility to get along without them. About 8 o'clock I reported to the Chief that I thought it would be impossible to retain our position much longer, as the lines had been broken. I was directed to rally the men and make another effort. There was a space cleared in front of the theatre, the people having left to avoid the stones. After this I went on the 8th Street side, and found one or two hundred young men and boys stoning the building. I attempted to make an arrest of one but was beaten back by the mob and had to run for my life. After finding that the line had been broken up, I went to the Astor Place side. I got inside with difficulty. I found the Chief, the Recorder, General Sandford and the Sheriff, I reported to them that I thought it was impossible for the police to keep the crowd back—that they would demolish the building unless we were reinforced.

Had the crowd at this moment tried to enter the building, they would no doubt have succeeded. Luckily, they were satisfied to continue the stoning and protest the half-dozen arrests made by the harried police before the military arrived. Although General Sandford's militia was in readiness and awaiting orders at the Washington Parade Ground (Washington Square), the building and the police had to sustain another half hour of attack before the messenger reached Sandford and the troops arrived.

They marched into Astor Place from Broadway and took up positions on the sidewalk in front of the theatre, their first objective being to clear the entrance so that those inside, whose fright now outweighed their curiosity, could leave the theatre unmolested. But the sight of the military, instead of subduing the street crowd, fired them to a new fury. If there had been up to now some tacit respect for the "stars," who were performing an unpleasant duty, and a disposition to regard the building as the chief target, there was no similar respect for soldiers interfering in civilian affairs. When the troops "defiled across the street for the purpose of clearing it and dispersing those who were throwing missiles into the building," they encountered a point-blank volley of stone. According to one report, "General Sandford was felled to the earth; Lieut. W. R. Harrison was badly wounded; and eleven out of the nineteen men in the first company were so severely injured as to be incapacitated for duty."

In the face of such a determined adversary, the militiamen informed the Sheriff that they would no longer stand to their duty if they had to hold fire. After a hasty conference and an unintelligible proclamation to the crowd ordering them to disperse at the peril of being shot, the troops were ordered to fire one volley over the heads of the attackers. This provided a temporarily dampening effect; but when it became apparent that no one had been injured, and when the rumor took hold that the soldiers had fired blank cartridges, a new blast of paving stones was lofted at the defenders.

For a moment it was hoped that this might be the last desperate charge before a retreat, but it was soon clear that the fury of the crowd was far from being exhausted. The fatal command to fire point-blank into the mob was finally given. Two men fell. The first was shot in the arm; the sec-

GREAT RIOT AT THE ASTOR PLACE OPERA HOUSE, NEW YORK.

Courtesy of the New York Historical Society, N. Y. C.

ond, hit in the right cheek of his face, was killed. With just
two down after a full volley, it was evident that a large share
of the soldiers had ignored the order. And when they now
saw the first clear evidence of retreat, they found comfort
in their disobedience. But the disposition of the crowd was
misjudged. A few retreating steps, a moment to rally forces,
and the attack was renewed with increased vigor and rage.
Another volley killed half a dozen and injured as many
more. Another retreat provided an interval long enough for
the military to establish a line across the street at both ends
of Astor Place to prevent any connection between Broadway
and the Bowery. (The same maneuver had been accomplished earlier on Eighth Street.) The mob meantime had
congregated in the area between the Opera House and the
junction of Fourth Avenue and the Bowery and were rallying themselves for another charge. With both sides now
joined in almost continual firing, General Sandford—still
out of action but observing the bloody scene—dispatched an
order for more troops and "two brass pieces loaded with
grape." At 11:30 the reinforcements arrived and set up their
cannons in front of the theatre. Though the action was subsiding, it was after midnight before the firing stopped completely. The sad assessment was now begun. But with such
disorganization in both camps and with so many unattached
spectators caught in the fire, the full casualty list was not
completed for several days.

The final tabulation recorded thirty-one casualties (twenty-two were killed in the course of the rioting) and somewhat over a hundred wounded. The seeds of a misunderstanding between two actors, "Ned" Forrest and W. C.
Macready, had been planted twenty-three years before, and
the resulting quarrel had culminated in the worst riot in the
history of the theatre.

Actors and Riots

Riots were not new to the theatre in 1849, nor were feuding actors, but neither had ever led to, or been connected with, such bloody consequences. A twentieth-century view of such past disturbances inevitably focuses on their seemingly inconsequential nature. The stakes appear to have been too large for the game. We ask what was gained by all the shouting and shooting? Yet we still howl, if we don't shoot, when our sensibilities are jarred. We picket a singer or deport a pianist for his or her wartime sympathies, black-list an actor for his political allegiance, boycott a movie for its immoral or irreligious episodes. But our protests are more genteel. Rarely do they get fired up to riotous action.

The respected New Yorker of 1849, not the man in the street, deplored the Astor Place violence, but he recognized that such things could and did happen. Even the more elegant theatres could not always maintain an atmosphere congenial to their well-bred patrons. Nor was an audience with fine society markings a certain guarantee, in New York City or anywhere else, of a dignified theatrical evening.

In 1721, at the Lincoln's Inn Theatre in London, on the occasion of another *Macbeth,* a spectator walked across the stage in front of the actors to speak with a friend who was seated on the opposite side. Noblemen were permitted stage seats, to be handier to the actresses. This eighteenth-century gentleman, a heavy consumer of usquebaugh who was said to have been in a state of intoxication for six years, was intercepted by the theatre manager, who protested the unseemly interruption of the play. The manager was rewarded with a blow in the face which he immediately returned. The noblemen on the stage then rushed to the defense of their elegant brother and would certainly have destroyed the poor manager had not the actors joined the battle. A freewheeling brawl ensued with the entire audience participating, and before the military arrived, the furniture and the hangings of the boxes had been slashed by swords, mirrors and mouldings smashed, and lighted torches "hurled amongst the scenery." The theatre had to be closed for a week and a guard posted to prevent any further outbreak. The Lincoln's Inn Theatre and its patrons had been the innocent victims of a previous disorderly action in 1679. Two cavaliers had entered the theatre and tried to set it on fire to smoke out their detested enemy, the Duchess of Portland, who was attending the performance.

The ill-advised conduct of the management provoked a riot at the Haymarket Theatre, in London, in 1737. With England and France at odds, a company of French comedians could hardly have expected a very cordial reception on an English stage, but the Haymarket manager, to his sorrow, took the risk. When the curtain went up, the actors were showered with "bad fruit, rotten eggs, and other missiles." Those few in the audience who arrived without ammunition tore at the furnishings and jeered the French and Spanish ambassadors, who were in attendance. These gentlemen, finally escaping to the street, found that the rioters had cut the traces of their coaches, "in order to make sure of the honour of their company." Order was finally restored with the assistance of the military and a magistrate who invoked the Riot Act.

In 1740 another riot occurred in London, at the Drury Lane Theatre. Madame Chateauneuf had been engaged as the *premiere danseuse,* and a full house had been drawn to see her. When she failed to appear and no apology was heard from the manager, the spectators smashed the orchestral instruments, tore up the benches in the pit, broke the chandeliers, and pulled down the royal arms.

In 1747 an argument between Thomas Sheridan, father of Richard Brinsley, and a young man named Kelly led to some mob mayhem upon Mr. Kelly at a theatre in Dublin. Kelly had climbed on the stage and insulted one of the actresses, forcing her to retreat to her dressing room. Sheridan, acting as her protector, had, in the course of the argument, broken Kelly's nose. The next night Kelly turned up at the theatre with a number of his friends and was met by a body of students from Trinity College, who were on hand to protect the lady and the management. "For several nights," as one reporter described it, "the theatre was converted into a battle-field, in which swords, cudgels, and other weapons were freely used. The undergraduates took several of the opposing faction prisoners and carried them off to the College where they inflicted condign punishment upon them, with, it is said, the approval of their provost." Finally the justices ordered the theatre closed, and the altercation ended in the law courts with Kelly condemned to three-months' imprisonment and fined five hundred pounds.

The Haymarket manager had further troubles in 1749, this time for failing to present the announced attraction. Posters had advertised that on a specified evening a member of the company was "to put himself into a quart bottle." The theatre was packed, but the shriveling expert failed to appear. When the enraged audience was quieted, the manager assured them that his performer would positively appear the next evening and in retribution for his bad faith would use a pint instead of a quart bottle. The next night the routine was repeated, but before the manager could announce half a pint for the next evening, the audience realized that they had been duped. The Duke of Cumberland rose from his box as furious as the rest of the crowd and, with his sword drawn, directed the infuriated mob to destroy everything within reach. Everyone seemed glad to oblige. The decorative trappings were ripped out, carried into the street, and thrown onto a large bonfire. It was later discovered that this expensive hoax had originated in the whimsical brain of the Duke of Montague.

Even such a popular actor-manager as David Garrick had some trouble with a disapproving public. In 1754 he attempted to brave the antagonism of the Francophobes with a burlesque called "The Chinese Festival," which employed the services of several French performers. He had been warned that the pit would not tolerate their presence on the

stage, but aristocratic patrons assured him of their support,
so Garrick determined to defy the patriots. At the first performance, the presence of the King restricted them to groans,
hisses, and catcalls; but on the next night their resentment
no longer restrained, they loudly and insistently demanded
that the French actors leave the stage. The aristocrats' answer to this was that the performance must be continued as
planned. Garrick was caught in the middle, as were the
trembling actors. The gentlemen in the boxes, cheered and
directed by their ladies, dropped into the pit with their
swords drawn and engaged the commoners. But in spite of
the blood that was spilled in this initial assault, the "pittites"
won the battle and cleared the theatre after destroying everything within reach. Inspirited by their victory and unsati-
ated by the damage done, they marched to Garrick's house
in Southampton Street and demolished the windows with
stones.

Garrick was the victim of a second disturbance six years
later, when he tried to abolish the customary half-price admission after the third act. It had been a long-standing custom to permit latecomers to see the last two acts and the
afterpiece at half-rates. The first performance following this
announcement met with a violent uproar of protest from the
entire audience. One drunken spectator carrying a torch
reached the stage and tried to set fire to the scenery but was
prevented by the actor Moody (no kin to the writer). The
howls were so deafening that Garrick was obliged to ring
down the curtain and refund the evening's receipts. At the
opening of the performance the next night, the audience
rose in a body and with Fitzpatrick, the critic, as their
spokesman demanded to know "if Garrick was prepared to
accede to their wishes and abolish his obnoxious innova-
tion." Garrick had learned his lesson; he gave in. But the

house was not satisfied. They insisted that Moody apologize
for having dared to lay hands on a "gentleman." Moody,
thinking to put the audience in a good humour, remarked
with a strong Hibernian accent that "he was sorry he had
displeased them by saving their lives in putting out the fire."
He misjudged the audience; they were not amused. They
insisted that the actor beg their pardon upon his knees.
When he refused, the tumult began again; whereupon Garrick came forward and assured them that Moody should not
appear on the stage again as long as he displeased them. The
audience had won their point, and Fitzpatrick magnani-
mously informed Garrick a few days later that they were
now willing to let Moody resume his part.

In 1809 the Haymarket Theatre was again the scene of an
odd audience protest. The production of a burlesque, *The
Tailors; or, the Tragedy for Warm Weather,* roused the
wrath of the "knights of the thimble and bodkin." Infuriated at the lampooning that they received in the play, they
addressed themselves to the manager, demanding alterations
in the text. When their insistent petitions and threatening
letters were ignored, the "knights" appeared in mass at a
performance. The first intimation of any irregularity was
noted when someone threw a pair of scissors at the head of
one of the actors. This was followed by other sewing-room
missiles, and it was not until magistrates, police, and finally
military guards were called in that the disturbance was
quieted down and the ringleaders arrested.

Probably the most widely reported theatrical disturbances
were the O. P. (Old Prices) Riots, which took place in London at the new Covent Garden Theatre in the fall of 1809.
The year before, just a week after the opening of the season,
the old Covent Garden had burned to the ground. A new
structure on the same site was put up at a "hand-gallop, with-

out check, without control, without superintendence" and
was ready for use in September, 1809. Even before the *pre-
mière* was announced, the public registered their dissatisfaction with the reconstruction. The management was trying to
crowd too many customers into the dismal, barn-like edifice.
The popular galleries had been reduced in size to make room
for twenty-six private boxes which, with their private staircases and entrances, would certainly attract the ladies of the
town and "make the place commodious for their corrupt de-
signs." Finally, one week before the gala opening, the public
was advised of a price advance: from six to seven shillings for
the boxes and from three and six to fourpence for the pit. As
if this were not enough, a foreigner—an Italian soprano
named Madame Catalani—had been engaged to augment the
dramatic company and at the exorbitant fee of seventy-five
pounds a night. Accordingly, when the doors opened (at five
o'clock on September 18, 1809) for the performance of *Macbeth,* the circumstances were decidedly inauspicious. With
the prices raised, the number of private boxes increased, and
a foreigner on the pay roll, John Kemble and his company
should have been primed for trouble.

The hooting started when the band struck up "God Save
the King," rumbled on at a low key through the choral
rendering of "Rule Britannia," and broke loose in earnest as
Kemble stepped forward to deliver the prologue which
Horace Twiss had composed for the occasion. "Old Prices!
No Catalani! Off! Off! Old Prices!" were about all that could
be heard. Shakespeare's lines were treated no more respectfully than those of Twiss. Even the stately Mrs. Siddons, the
Lady Macbeth, was completely drowned out by the uproar.
The lavish embellishment of the production, so carefully
and expensively prepared to enrapture the audience, served
only to nettle them more. One spectator, raging at the sight

of the five-hundred-pounds' worth of costumes worn by
Kemble and his sister, Mrs. Siddons, remarked that "it was
to feed this vanity, and to pay an Italian singer, that the public was screwed." Through the entire play and the afterpiece
not a word was heard from the stage. Most of the audience
stood with their hats on, many of them with their backs to
the stage, and chanted, "Old Prices, Old Prices!" No damage
was done to the house, however, nor were the actors mo-
lested. After the company had completed their dumb-show
exercise, Kemble made the mistake of summoning a pair
of Bow Street constables to the stage. The sight of these
minions was the final affront, and the decibel count climbed
higher than ever. Only after the constables had left the stage
and the audience had been permitted a final unintimidated
outburst, were they willing to join in "God Save the King"
and depart.

The next morning the London *Times* came out in support of the popular demand, and at about the same time
Kemble must have consulted his journal entry of 1791:
"Whenever there is Danger of a Riot always act an Opera;
for Musick drowns the Noise of Opposition." *The Beggar's
Opera* was announced for the second night. If the audience
heard the music, they were certainly not soothed. Placards,
banners, and posters were hoisted throughout the house, all
supporting the vocal demand for "Old Prices." At the end of
the performance, the howling having again drowned out the
actors for the entire evening, the crowd moved toward the
front of the house. There, however, they were faced with a
line-up of the constabulary and the gaping openings of the
trap doors, which were expected to serve as man-traps for
the attackers. The audience then retreated to their places and
concluded their shouting from a proper distance.

On the next night Cooke's *Richard III* supplied the accom-

paniment for the O. P. demands. At the conclusion of the
farce, Kemble ventured forward to address the mob, and for
the first time in three nights some words from the stage
were heard. He pleaded and cajoled, spoke of the increased
production costs and of the poor return that the management
had received on its investment, and praised the fairness and
magnanimity of the English audience. Every statement was
met with a derisive howl. Finally, and as if he did not know
what answer he would get, he shouted, "Ladies and gentlemen, I wait to know what you want." The reply came in
chorus, the same cry that had been ringing in his ears for
three days: "Old Prices."

Covent Garden was now under siege. Night after night
the plays went on in dumb show. The shouts became louder
and the action more daring. Constables took up permanent
stations at the front of the house, the trap doors were left
open, fire engines were arranged on stage, and professional
fighters, hired by the managers, were spotted among the
audience. Inevitably the catcalls and placards became more
abusive and the physical encounters more frequent.

On the sixth night Kemble came forward to speak again.
He proposed that a committee of impartial citizens examine
the account books of Covent Garden and issue a detailed
report to the public. For the first time in six days Kemble's
words were received without protest. While the five judges—
John Sylvester, Sir Thomas Plomer, John Whitmore, J. J.
Angerstein, and Sir Charles Price—checked over the figures,
the house was darkened, and the rival forces were allowed
to cool off. Six days later the committee announced its find-
ings. In six years of operation the Covent Garden management had maintained a fair and reasonable return of six and
three-eighths per cent on their investment. With the new
building, unless the new prices were allowed, they stood to

lose three fourths of one per cent. The price advance should
be allowed.

The O. P. forces were, as might have been anticipated, un-
moved by talk of percentages and profits. Kemble got his
first answer from the *Statesman,* which announced: "This
is precisely what we expected. We were confident that the
proprietors would *perplex* the Committee, the public—by
talking about the *rate of interest*. What have the public to
do with the rate of interest upon an *imaginary* capital?"
When the theatre opened again, on October 4, Kemble
faced an opposition loaded with heaver ammunition. A
battery of placards announced the enormous and ill-gotten
profits taken by the management during the preceding years,
using figures lifted from the committee's report. The O. P.
contingent, rejuvenated by the cooling-off period and their
voices tuned up, were ready to shout till their protests were
heeded and the old prices restored.

Macready, then a boy of sixteen, was in London serving
his actor's apprenticeship by attending all the theatres. Being
on the free-list at Covent Garden, he got a view of the O. P.
disturbances, and undoubtedly his recollection of these
events flashed back to him on the stage of the Astor Place
Opera House forty years later. His *Reminiscences* provides
one of the best contemporary records of the O. P. rioters'
nightly routine.

The spirit of resistance was persevering and indomitable. After
three or four weeks the tumult became so far lulled that the three
first acts of each performance were listened to by the scanty audiences that attended; but at half-price the well-organized opposition rushing in, began the O. P. dance on the benches of the pit,
and not one syllable more was to be heard. The scenes presented
by the acting audience, and the "hubbub wild" that deafened the
ear, baffle description. Some of the leading pugilists of the day

were ranked in the boxes, to champion the cause of the proprietors where the *mêlée* might be thickest. Horns, catcalls, and all imaginable discordant sounds were mingled in the vast uproar.

Nor did the mobsters limit their activities to the theatre. Medals were struck off representing Kemble as a donkey with John Bull on his back, special O. P. dances were composed, and hatbands with "O. P." printed on them became fashionable. Numerous songs and verses appeared in dishonor of "Black Jack," as Kemble was now known. The rioters gathered in front of his elegant house in Great Russell Street, and though usually satisfied with verbal protestations, on one occasion smashed the parlor windows. Kemble, now fearing the worst, had ladders placed against the windows facing the garden, to facilitate a hasty retreat if his residence were stormed. He pleaded with the newspapers to adopt a more temperate view, but without success. Nevertheless, after the weeks of ego-shattering dumb-show performances before hostile audiences, he was still unwilling to admit defeat.

Finally, in December, 1809, a court action forced him to submit to the rioters' demands. Henry Clifford, a barrister who had been one of the O. P. principals from the beginning, was arrested after a performance at the insistence of James Brandon, the venerable box keeper of Covent Garden. Clifford was taken forcibly to Bow Street Station but was immediately dismissed. Seeing his chance to bring the whole dispute to a head, Clifford immediately filed a charge of assault and false imprisonment against Brandon. When the case was brought before Sir James Mansfield in the Court of Common Pleas on December 5, Clifford's attorney, a Mr. Best, centered his plea on three points:

(1) Noise and uproar at a theatre were to be expected; there could have been no riot where there had been no damage.

(2) If his client had committed a misdemeanor, he must be arrested at the scene and not after he departed from the theatre.

(3) A larger question of moral cause, a clear case of oppression and tyranny, was before the court.

As might have been expected, the judge sided with Brandon and the management; but the people's jury, after ten minutes of deliberation, decided in Clifford's favor. Although the jury allowed damages of only five pounds instead of the one hundred that had been asked, the court's verdict was unmistakable. Any continuation of the O. P. battle was clearly futile as far as Kemble was concerned. The riots were over.

On December 14, five hundred "real friends of the Drama and reprobators of Managerial insolence and brutality" banqueted at the Crown and Anchor Tavern. Clifford was the toastmaster and Kemble the principal speaker. Under the circumstances any submission would have been humiliating, but Kemble, stubborn to the end, rendered his in the lofty and superior tone that he had maintained from the beginning. He did apologize, however, for "hiring Ruffians" and then declared that all suits against the rioters would be dropped, that Brandon would be dismissed, and, hardest of all, that the old prices would be restored. John Bull had won.

The theatre public was master; the actor servant. Even star billing on the marquee did not grant any disregard for public interest, and riots were the ultimate reminder to a recalcitrant actor. Kemble learned his lesson in 1809, as did Edmund Kean in 1821.

The oubreaks against Kean in Boston, first in 1821 and again in 1825, were not his only encounters with a disapproving public, but they were the first riot-like disturbances in the American theatre. Kean had determined to wind up his

1821 American tour in Boston, where he had played to enthusiastic houses in February. The manager had advised him
that in late May most of the patrons of the Boston theatre
would have gone to the country, but Kean insisted on the
engagement. His first and second nights drew fair houses,
but when Kean looked through the curtain at seven o'clock
on the third night, he counted only twenty heads. He
stormed out of the theatre and back to his hotel, and even
when he was advised later that the crowd had increased, he
refused to return. On the next day the abuses of the scorned
patrons appeared in the Boston press, and when they were
repeated in the New York papers a few days later, Kean
issued a reply in the New York *National Advocate*. His sarcastic observation that Boston audiences visited the theatre
only during certain favorable months of the year and then
only through curiosity rather than from any genuine appre-
ciation of dramatic talent, added coals to the fire that he had
started and kept it smouldering until he returned to Boston
in 1825. Before returning, however, he became well acquainted with the authority of unfriendly audiences in his
own country. An ill-considered affair with the wife of a
London alderman, resulting in an alienation suit, put Kean
in the bad graces of his English public. He was hooted from
the stage in Edinburgh, and in London he played in "blind
shows," unable to make himself heard above the protests of
the spectators. These hostilities drove him back to America.
But if he had forgotten the tirades that had issued from
Boston in 1821, the Bostonians had not forgotten him. At
his first appearance in December, 1825, he was showered
with a "fusilade of missiles both hard and soft," and was
driven from the stage by the "mobocratic rowdies." He, like
Kemble, was forced to an embarrassing apology. In a letter
(December 21, 1825) to the citizens of Boston he wrote,

"Acting from the impulse of irritation, I certainly was disrespectful to the Boston public; calm deliberation convinces me I was wrong. The first step towards the throne of mercy is confession."

No doubt many of these disturbances would have been forestalled if certain concessions had been made; but theatrical stars, endowed with more than a reasonable share of arrogance, stubbornness, and temper, yield neither gracefully nor easily. Macready and Forrest were no exceptions to this rule. Macready, who was tormented by self-doubts, frequently offended his colleagues with his haughty tone and overbearing manner, and Forrest had a turbulent nature that occasionally erupted in displays of violence. Neither imagined, however, that this personal rivalry would terminate in a riot.

At the present writing, more than a century later, the reasons for the disaster are not immediately evident. After all, the O. P. riots had gone on for sixty-one nights without any fatal injury to the participants or serious damage to the theatre, and the Astor Place riot might have been expected to follow a similar, if less protracted, course. Why, then, did it develop as it did? Part of the explanation is to be found in the lengthy build-up that came before the final event. The preceding period of professional rivalry and open hostility between Forrest and Macready had lasted for some twenty-three years.

Forrest and Macready

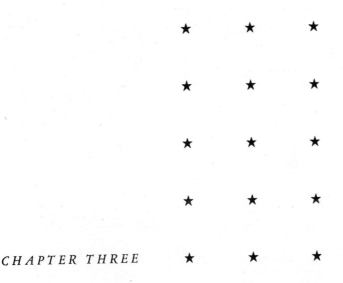

The two actors took up their positions in opposite corners as early as 1826, when Macready made his first American tour. During the fall season of that year both were appearing in New York. Forrest was the chief attraction at the "democratic" Bowery Theatre, while Macready was at the "aristocratic" Park. There was no demonstration of open animosity between the two men, but they were competing for audience favor. Macready did not then, nor did he ever, consider Forrest to be in the same class. Unenlightened American audiences might venture some comparisons, but these could not be taken seriously.

EDWIN FORREST

Macready recorded his first impressions of Forrest after seeing him as Mark Antony in W. A. Conway's production of *Julius Caesar* in December, 1826. He was struck by Forrest's "vehemence and rude force," but also by the fact that "he had not rightly understood some passages in the text." The best that he could say was that Forrest "was possessed of natural requisites in no ordinary degree" and might with "careful discipline" make a tolerable actor. He was certain, however, that Forrest would never develop this self-discipline. "The injudicious and ignorant flattery, and the facetious applause of his supporters, the 'Bowery lads' as they were termed, in low-priced theatres, would fill his purse, would blind him to his deficiency in taste and judgment, and satisfy his vanity, confirming his self-opinion of attained perfection." These views must be treated with a degree of skepticism, for they were reminiscences written after Macready's final unhappy visit to America in 1849. In 1826 he had not yet begun his diary.

Macready was on the right track in his appraisal of Forrest's patrons although he was predisposed to down-grade the Bowery audience. A more accurate and unprejudiced view is to be found in Walt Whitman's contemporary account.

Recalling from that period the occasion of either Forrest or Booth, any good night at the old Bowery, packed from ceiling to pit with its audience mainly of alert, well-dress'd, full-blooded young and middle-aged men, the best average of American born mechanics—the emotional nature of the whole mass arous'd by the power and magnetism of as mighty mimes as ever trod the stage—the whole crowded auditorium, and what seeth'd in it, and flash'd from its faces and eyes, to me as much a part of the show as any—bursting forth in one of those long-kept-up tempests of handclapping peculiar to the Bowery—no dainty kid-glove business, but electric force and muscle from perhaps two thousand full-sinew'd men—(the inimitable and chromatic tempest of one of those ovations to Edwin Forrest, welcoming him back after an absence, comes up to me this moment)—such sounds and scenes as here resumed will surely afford to many old New Yorkers some fruitful recollections.

Forrest was a robust and high-spirited player. He felt comfortably at home with these Bowery devotees, whereas he could never bear the chilly criticism of the "polite society" at the Park. Macready was at the opposite pole. Untutored enthusiasm, no matter how vociferous, could not be accepted in preference to the discriminating applause, no matter how feeble, of the cultured few.

Although, in 1826, the respective managements of the Park and Bowery placed the two actors in opposition, there was no external evidence of any personal animosity between Macready and Forrest, nor, in fact, any evidence that the two met during this engagement. Professionally, they were not yet quite in the same category. Macready was already a star; Forrest was just becoming one. It was not until the following year, when Forrest's salary took the phenomenal jump from forty dollars a week to two hundred a night that he approached the peak of his celebrity.

Only one incident during the 1826-27 tour hinted at the anti-Macready feeling that was to develop later. In Philadelphia Macready reviled a property man for supplying arrows (for *William Tell*) of "inferior American quality." A stream of letters to the newspapers denounced Macready for this insult, and he was obliged to apologize to the company. The matter ended there, and he continued his engagement without further incident. In the spring he returned to England.

For the next ten years each actor stuck to his own territory.

WILLIAM C. MACREADY

Forrest, with his muscular and exuberant style and his fervent devotion to the cause of American democracy, took up a commanding position as an actor and citizen of the first rank. In 1828, he announced the first of his playwriting contests for American dramatists writing on native themes. The initial invitation in the *Critic* for November 22, 1828, read: "To the author of the best Tragedy, in five acts, of which the hero or principal character shall be an aboriginal of this country, the sum of five hundred dollars, and half of the proceeds of the third representation, with my own gratuitous services on that occasion. The award to be made by a committee of literary and theatrical gentlemen." *Metamora,* by John Augustus Stone, received the first prize and was immediately added to Forrest's repertoire. In similar fashion in succeeding years he took on eight other plays by American dramatists. Forrest's motives in these contests may not have been exclusively altruistic and patriotic, but that he held a burning passion for America and democratic ideals cannot be doubted.

When in July, 1834, he announced his intention of leaving the stage for two years to seek enlargement and perfection in taste and judgment through foreign travel, he was honored by an elaborate testimonial banquet. Among the illustrious subscribers—all friends and admirers of Forrest—were Washington Irving, George P. Morris, J. Fenimore Cooper, and William Gilmore Simms. These and others—Mayor Cornelius Lawrence was on the guest of honor's right— heard Forrest praise his "native land," which, he vowed, would always be in his heart no matter what "classic soil" he might tread upon. He kept to his word. In Genoa he went aboard an American warship and before greeting the commander, dropped to his knees and folded the "star-spangled flag to his lips." Of his presentation to King Louis Phillippe,

he wrote, "I entered, and made my debut before the King of
France with not half the trepidation I experienced on pre-
senting myself for the first time before a *sovereign* in New
York—I mean the sovereign people."

During his two years of sponging up culture in Rome,
Naples, Genoa, Turin, Geneva, Paris, Hamburg, St. Peters-
burg, Moscow, Constantinople, Athens, London, and Strat-
ford-on-Avon, Forrest never appeared on the stage. Just before departing for home in August, 1836, he considered the
possibility of a Drury Lane engagement for the following
October; but, although he had been impressed by English
hospitality—particularly that of his future in-laws, the Sinclairs—he felt that there might be some prejudice against an
American player on the English stage. He made few ac-
quaintances among the theatrical folk and seems not to have
seen Macready in the theatre or out.

Back in New York he was welcomed as a returning hero
with a glittering and profitable engagement at the Park.
Foreign travel had made this fashionable playhouse appear
less objectionable. For six performances he received the
unheard-of sum of $3,000, high honor indeed. Forrest, well
aware that the premium prices resulted from the rumors of
his impending London appearance, explained to his patrons
in a curtain speech that he had not sought the London engagement. He finally had consented "not for my own sake,
for my ambition is satisfied with the applauses of my own
countrymen, but partly in compliance with the wishes of a
number of American friends, and partly to solve a doubt
which is entertained by many of our citizens, whether Eng-
lishmen would receive an American actor with the same
favor which is here extended to them. But, whatever may be
the result, the approbation of that public which first stamped
the native dramatist and actor will ever be my proudest

recollection." The audience cheered. Forrest was their favorite, and it was time, as he said, that the British should be
given a chance to see a truly American theatrical product.
Too many English actors had been thriving on the servile
obeisance of American audiences and on American cash.
Forrest departed, in September, 1836, as American stage
missionary extraordinary to John Bull's island.

Through no fault or contriving on his own, Forrest caught
Macready at a touchy moment and under irritating circumstances. Forrest appeared at Drury Lane under the management of Alfred Bunn. Macready had just quit Drury Lane
and was at Covent Garden as a result of a quarrel with Bunn.
The previous April, some unaccountable managerial whim
had led Bunn to announce Macready in a Shakespearian
bastardization, "The three first acts of *Richard III."* Macready, whose indignation at this affront was widely supported by his friends, was brought to the breaking point on
the night of April 29. He had played the three first acts of
Richard III "in a sort of desperate way, with spirits depressed
and overweighed by the situation," and was, as he says in his
diary, returning from the stage.

It is not easy to describe the state of pent-up feeling of anger,
shame, and desperate passion that I endured. As I came off the
stage, ending the third act of "Richard," in passing by Bunn's door
I opened it, and unfortunately he was there. I could not contain
myself; I exclaimed, "You damned scoundrel! How dare you use
me in this manner," and going up to him as he sat on the other
side of the table I struck him as he rose, a backhanded slap across
the face. I did not hear what he said, but I dug my fist into him
as effectively as I could; he caught hold of me, and got at one
time the little finger of my left hand in his mouth, and bit it. I
exclaimed, "You rascal! Would you bite." He shouted out "Mur-

der! Murder!" and after some little time several persons came into
the room. I was then upon the sofa, the struggle having brought
us right round the table. Willmott, the prompter, said to me, "Sir,
you had better go to your room, you had better go to your room."

If Macready had been outraged at Bunn's behavior, he was
infuriated and shamed by his own intemperate outburst. "No
one can more severely condemn my precipitation than myself. No enemy can censure me more harshly, no friend
lament more deeply my forgetfulness of all I ought to have
thought upon." For days his diary echoed this self-castiga-
tion: "I can never, never, during my life, forgive myself."

This was the first time Macready had completely lost his
control, but he had always been painfully self-conscious
about his intolerant attitudes toward his inferiors. Macready,
an unyielding but suffering aristocrat, was repeatedly pained
by the fact that his superior airs were so frequently taken
for rudeness. It is "not vanity that makes me case myself in
pride, but a consciousness of not having won a secure title to
distinction, and the nervous and unquiet apprehension of its
being questioned." At another time he wrote, "Why is it that
in society I so often have the pleasure of receiving marked
attention and particular courtesy, and that my acquaintance
is so little sought—so little, as to make me think myself
either disagreeable in manner or dull in conversation." This
kind of self-analysis recurred in the diary time and again.
Inconsequential demonstrations of uncouth behavior would
send him into absurd tantrums. Of a *King Lear* rehearsal in
1834, he wrote, "... in a very bad temper; ridiculous as it is,
the cause of it: the sight of my neat book in the dirty prompter's hands."

Possessed of such a touchy temper, and still feeling the
sting of a popular judgment against him in favor of Bunn,

Macready could not be expected to regard Forrest with kindness. Yet, surprisingly enough, he did, or pretended to. Undoubtedly he feared to let his natural feelings have sway, mindful of the unpleasant self-recrimination that might follow. On October 15, 1836, two days before Forrest's opening at the Drury Lane, Macready noted in his diary, "Rose late, and canvassed with my counsel of the home department the best mode of arrangement in inviting Mr. Forrest to our home. Wrote a note of invitation to him."

In planning his London engagement Forrest had wished to provoke comparison, and risk opposition, immediately with his rendering of *Othello,* but his friends urged him to the safer course of easing his way into the graces of the English audience. He chose then to make the opening, on October 17, an all-American evening with his performance of Spartacus in Dr. Robert Montgomery Bird's *The Gladiator.* The tactic seems to have been well-advised. Critics condemned the play but were taken by Forrest's strikingly muscular figure and powerful voice. The London *Chronicle* wrote the next day, "Victory sits perched upon his beaver, and he must and will support her without losing a single feather." Even as skeptical a reviewer as Macready's friend, John Forster, found "no levity, no feebleness, no indifference in his [Forrest's] manner." The judgments for Forrest were tentatively favorable; the final evaluation would be given after the critics had heard him in Shakespeare.

Within the week Forrest undertook *Othello.* The notices, excepting those of Forster, spoke rapturously of "the most promising tragedian that has appeared in our day," and rated his performance "among the very best displays that the stage in this country can boast of." With most of the critics cheering the American actor, it was small comfort to Macready to read Forster on Forrest: "given to little fierce bursts of pas-

FORREST AS SPARTACUS

sions . . . no intellectual comprehension of what he was about." These were trying days for Macready. At his own rehearsal of *Othello* on October 21, he was "depressed by finding myself not possessed with the character of Othello, and annoyed by the carelessness of the people about the arrangement of the last scene." On the twenty-fourth, when Forster and Dow brought him a first-hand report on Forrest, he willingly admitted that it "would be stupid and shallow hypocrisy to say that I was indifferent to the result. It is of great importance to me to retain my superiority, and my wishes for his success follow the desire I have to be considered above him! Is this illiberal? I hope not. Their accounts [i.e., Forster's and Dow's] of his performance have certainly reduced very much my opinion of his mind, which, from the particulars they related, cannot be of the highest order." Macready had to have something for self-assurance.

Forrest came to call at Macready's home, "Elstree," on Sunday, October 30. Macready, impersonating the gracious host, evidently managed well enough to convince even himself. He presented Forrest to all his friends, among them T. N. Talfourd, author of *Ion,* and Robert Browning. He gave Forrest the honor of "taking Mrs. Macready down" and, as he reported in his diary that evening, found the whole occasion "agreeable and cheerful." Certainly Forrest detected no mockery or insincerity at "Elstree." He wrote to William Leggett of the New York *Evening Post*: "Mr. Macready has behaved in the handsomest manner to me. Before I arrived in England he had spoken of me in the most flattering terms, and on my arrival he embraced the earliest opportunity to call upon me, since which time he has extended to me many delicate courtesies and attention, all showing the native kindness of his heart and great refinement and good breeding."

On November 19, the Garrick Club gave a dinner in honor

of Forrest, and although five of the eighteen guests had already departed when Macready arrived and Talfourd's toast to Macready had to be repeated, Macready maintained his pose of kindly self-effacement. "I came to pay, not to receive, a compliment; and could assure my highly-talented friend that no one extended the hands of welcome to him more fervently or sincerely than myself, in doing which I only endeavoured to repay a small part of the debt of gratitude which had been heaped on me by the kindness of his countrymen." Macready's real feelings were, characteristically, hidden in the pages of his diary. On December 2 he wrote, ". . . uneasy, unhappy; my spirits in the lowest depth; no cheering prospect before me. My days flow by, and are bearing me to my grave the same worthless, sinful, wretched being that I have ever been—perhaps even worse than I have ever been."

Forrest concluded his London engagement on December 19 and set out on a tour of the provinces. From then until February, 1837, when Forrest began a return engagement at Drury Lane, Macready had the city to himself. Having had these quiet days in which to temper his mounting anxiety, he was resolved, even when Forrest came back to London, not to let his feelings run uncontrolled. On March 3, his birthday, Macready had a heart-to-heart talk with himself in his diary.

To-day I am forty-four years of age. Before I left my bed I gave my mind to long and earnest reflection on the occurrences of my past life—on the unhappiness which, in my portion of good and ill, had fallen to my lot, and of its cause. Most of it is to be traced to myself, to my own violent passions, to the want of self-direction and command under events which seemed at war with my interests or feeling. The necessity of renewing and increasing my efforts to subdue my will; to bring my irritable will under the strong curb of reason; to think less of myself in relation to others; to extirpate the envious and vindictive feelings which still lurk within my disposition; prayed to God to confirm me in my good resolves, and rose with a lighter heart than I have felt these many days.

Macready always took account of anniversary occasions to reappraise himself. On April 29, 1837, he wrote, "A year ago I was hurried into the intemperate and frenzied act of striking Mr. Bunn. My sufferings from compunction have been very great, not perhaps more than my folly has deserved; but I pray to God that I may never again so far forget what is due to His laws, to myself, and to society."

With these admonitions in force, Macready was prepared to maintain a kindly front toward Forrest, even to encouraging Forrest's marriage to the nineteen-year-old daughter of his friend, John Sinclair. Forrest had met Catherine Sinclair on his previous visit, and now, certain of himself and of her, he proposed marriage. There was only one difficulty. The Sinclairs, skeptical of what might happen to their daughter in a strange land, insisted that Forrest settle a marriage dower on her. But Forrest would have none of this barbarous aristocratic custom. The Sinclairs were firm. Only after an impassioned appeal from Catherine did they finally consent. How could they, for "this hateful settlement," deny her her happiness or embitter the memory of her first meeting with Forrest. "The impression he made was so instantaneous and so strong that I remember I whispered to myself, while a thrill ran through me, 'This is the handsomest man on whom my eyes have ever fallen.'" They were married at St. Paul's in June, 1837.

The second encounter between Forrest and Macready had ended in an atmosphere of temporary sweetness and light. Macready was happy to get his competitor out of the country and to do so under such gracious circumstances. Forrest was too engrossed with his new bride and the happy thoughts of introducing her to America not to take Macready's courtesies at their face value.

The Edinburgh Hiss

CHAPTER FOUR ★ ★ ★

Forrest returned with a fervent yearning for "the bright skies of my own free land," and with a hankering to desert the stage and jump into the political maelstrom. Undoubtedly his encounters with the British aristocracy had goaded him to this new ambition. Even before he left England the idea must have occurred to him, for Macready reported that Forrest had spoken to him about his "leaving the stage, and devoting himself to politics." Not a happy prospect in Macready's view. What would happen, he wondered, "if Forrest should become president!"

But if his political sights had really been set that high, Forrest would probably have been just as skeptical as Macready. He merely wished to enter as a minor player on the political scene, a chance that he finally got when he appeared as the principal speaker at the Democratic celebration at the Broadway Tabernacle on July 4, 1838. A few lines from this speech—lines that were undoubtedly supplied by his newspaper friend, William Leggett—illustrate the spellbinding quality of Forrest's political utterances: "We are here not to celebrate the birthday of a despot, but the birthday of a nation; not to bow down in senseless homage before a throne founded on the prostrate rights of man, but to stand erect in the conscious dignity of equal freedom and join forces in the loud acclaim now swelling from the grateful hearts of fifteen millions of men in acknowledgment of the glorious charter of liberty our fathers this day proclaimed to the world."

Forrest realized, however, that there was more to politics than platform appearances. When he was seriously proposed as a candidate to the House of Representatives, he refused, on the grounds that he was ill-equipped for and disinclined toward the day-to-day drudgery of politics. He preferred to devote his energies to his own profession and to exploit his democratic sentiments on the stage. Forrest's flight into politics was very brief, but he maintained a lively connection with political figures throughout most of his life. On May 20, 1844, just before leaving Cincinnati for Nashville, he wrote to his mother, "I hope to visit the brave old man [Andrew Jackson] at the Hermitage, whose health I am rejoiced to hear has much improved during the last month or two. May he be spared yet to witness the downfall of the reckless [Whig] party whose chief desire seems to be to benefit the few at the expense of the many."

On this pilgrimage Forrest's path nearly crossed that of

Macready. The latter, now back in the States, was in Cincinnati on April 23, 1844, on his way back to New York from New Orleans. Macready's second tour of America had begun in New York in September, 1843, and ended in Boston in October, 1844. Although during this year the two actors had many superficially pleasant encounters, the pattern for their final competition in 1849 was being more clearly defined.

Forrest was one of the first to receive Macready in New York in 1843. After a dinner on the third of October, Macready reported confidently to his diary: "Dined with Forrest; met a very large party, too large for comfort, but it was most kindly intended. Our day was very cheerful; I like all I see of Forrest very much. He appears a clear-headed, honest, kind man; what can be better?" Yet a week later, after performing in James Sheridan Knowles's *Virginius,* he was annoyed to face the spectre of Forrest's conditioning of American taste. "The audiences of the United States have been accustomed to exaggeration in all its forms, and have applauded what has been most extravagant; it is not therefore surprising that they should bestow such little applause on me, not having their accustomed cues."

Macready was not going to permit any direct comparisons if they could be avoided. When Mr. Marshall, the Philadelphia manager, proposed that Macready and Forrest appear on alternate nights in the same roles, Macready declined. But comparisons were inescapable, especially between his and Forrest's Macbeths. Repeatedly the American press dwelt on the superiorities of the American actor over his foreign rival. After a month of such annoying comment, Macready came out with one of his characteristically impetuous pronouncements. *"He* [Forrest] *is not an artist.* Let him be an American actor—and a great American actor—but keep on this side of the Atlantic, and no one will gainsay his comparative excellence."

Such imperious and ill-considered opinions were expressed on several occasions during Macready's second American tour, and not always were they directed at Forrest. In New Orleans in February, 1844, Macready renewed his acquaintance with Henry Clay and found him "kind, urbane, and cheerful." One month later in Mobile he stormed at Noah Ludlow, the Mississippi valley impressario, for announcing Henry Clay and W. C. Macready on the same playbill. This "high-hatted" strolling player, obsessed with his "aristocratic importance," as Ludlow described him, insisted that Clay's name be removed from the bill.

Ludlow managed most of the theatres in which both Macready and Forrest appeared in the Midwest and South. And although he deplored Macready's "artiness" and his "affected, inflexible and angular action," he had to admit that the English actor outdrew Forrest during this spring of 1844. In Mobile Macready averaged $455 nightly against $397 for Forrest, and in St. Louis Macready also held the edge, $422 to $269. In both of these engagements, however, Forrest followed on Macready's heels, and undoubtedly Forrest was rhetorically justified in insisting that before he arrived, Macready had already "drained the public purse."

During this tour of the country Macready was forever fulminating against the uncouth Americans. Their tastes were dull and undiscriminating. They had been so fed on undisciplined and untutored "nature" on the stage that they were unable to perceive the merits of a genuine actor. His only pleasure was to be found in the "natural" actor's failure at the box office. He was overjoyed, for example, to learn that Forrest had drawn a measly $200 house at a performance at

the Walnut Street Theatre in Philadelphia. "If it be so, he is
justly punished for his ungentlemanly conduct."

Macready returned to England in November, 1844. Back
on his home ground and counting up the £5,500 he had
taken from America—mostly from *Hamlet,* he said—he
had agreeably warm and pleasant recollections. Even Forrest
appeared less objectionable at this distance. On November
3, Mrs. Macready wrote to Forrest on her husband's behalf:
"Nothing has given me greater pleasure from America than
that which the relation of the hospitality and kindness Mr.
Macready has received from you, during his sojourn in New
York, has communicated. I only wish I had any means of
testifying my gratitude to you, for your great attention to
him; which has gratified him very much, and which is one
of the delightful things among the many, he will have to
reflect upon, in remembering his visit to your great country."
Thus a third meeting of Forrest and Macready had been
concluded without any real head-on conflict and with at least
this epistolary expression of good will.

But Macready retained exclusive command of his side of
the Atlantic for only two and a half months. In February,
1845, almost as if he were chasing his opponent to his lair,
Forrest set sail for his second professional visit to England.
He opened in *Othello* at the Princess Theatre on February
17. As on his previous visit, the majority press reaction was
favorable. The reviewers spoke of "a conception mellowed
by experience," "masterly design," a performance "more
chaste than heretofore." There were a few derogatory press
references to "his spasms of rage" and to "his lack of study";
but these were less upsetting to Forrest than the concerted
catcalls and hisses that seemed to arise with organized regu-
larity from various sections of the house. Such demonstra-

tions, he felt, could have resulted only from some devilishly devised plot to drive him from the stage.

Whether or not Macready had had a hand in preparing this kind of reception for Forrest at the Princess, he spoke with charitable delight of the misfortune. "I am truly sorry for him (without wishing him *great* success) and deeply sorry for his wife." On the subject of Forrest's proposed visit to Paris, he seems to have written with some secret authority. In his diary entry for March 2, 1845, he says "Called on Mr. and Mrs. Forrest, with whom were several people; to me he observed that he was going to Paris where he would be 'better appreciated than he is here.' I fancy *not*." The italics are Macready's. Perhaps he assumed that his own warm reception in Paris the previous January would automatically prejudice Forrest's chances there.

What actually happened has never been determined, but it is a matter of record that Forrest was turned down when he sought an engagement with Mr. Mitchell's English company in Paris and again (by Bulwer-Lytton) when he attempted to add *Richelieu* and *The Lady of Lyons* to his (Forrest's) repertoire. Lytton's refusal took the form of imposing impossible conditions; the plays could not be performed "for a less period than ten nights each, upon *a payment beforehand of fifty guineas for the two.*" This was certainly an unreasonable arrangement, particularly if there is any truth in the statement made by Maddox (manager of the Princess) to Macready that Forrest had acted at the Princess for *nothing*.

Faced with the apparent antagonism of these two close friends of Macready (Mitchell and Bulwer-Lytton), Forrest was also exposed to the unfriendly reactions of John Forster, Macready's literary adviser and agent, who described For-

rest's Macbeth as a "caricature" and his Lear as a "roaring
pantaloon." It was therefore not unreasonable that Forrest
should identify Macready as the evil manipulator.

Late in 1848, when the quarrel between the two actors was
reaching a showdown, Macready attempted to explain away
his suspected connections with the earlier incidents by elicit-
ing a series of whitewash letters from his friends. In a letter
from London, dated December 14, 1848, Mitchell offered a
repetitive "decidedly not" to Macready's series of questions:
"Did I caution you *not* to allow Mr. Forrest to appear?" "Did
I throw obstacles of any kind in the way of Mr. Forrest's
appearance under your management in the Theatre at
Paris?" On November 26, in the same year, Bulwer-Lytton
had added his testimony: "I can truly say, that you never
directly or indirectly expressed even the remotest wish, that
Mr. Forrest should not act in any play of mine." But Macready evidently regarded this first reply as too tame. He drew
another letter from Bulwer-Lytton on December 16 that
answered his questions in order and with more vigor: "1st.
You never, directly or indirectly, through yourself or others,
expressed any wish whatsoever, that Mr. Forrest should not
perform in any play of mine. 2d. You never had any communication, direct or indirect, with me, or any agent of mine,
respecting any application from Mr. Forrest to act in my
plays. 3dly. I do not believe you capable of any interference
to the prejudice of the interests of another actor upon such
a point." The second letter went on for two pages in this
manner and concluded reassuringly: "I have that confidence
in the American public, that I feel perfectly persuaded, it will
rally around you, with regret and even shame at so unworthy
a calumny from a part of its population, unhappily misled.
I can conceive, that your high sense of honour may be
wounded at the mere suspicion of practices so foreign to your

nature. In England, the injustice of such attacks seems as ludicrously glaring, as if we had heard a report, that the Duke of Wellington had been broken for cowardice, or the Archbishop of Canterbury sent to the Treadmill for picking pockets." But these letters, written three years after the events, bear less weight than the face value of the immediate circumstances.

There is no final evidence to support the claim of Forrest's followers that Macready hired the "groaners" who disrupted Forrest's London performances in 1845. Indeed there are only hints and the circumstantial force of Macready's close association with Mitchell, Forster, and Bulwer-Lytton. But one does find in Macready's diary during the following twelve months (until the Edinburgh incident in March, 1846) the kind of self-reproach that Macready was addicted to after he had caught himself in an uncharitable act. Of course, during this period Macready had other troubles. His own engagements were not going well. Another American, Charlotte Cushman, was draining off more than her share of the London audience. Helen Faucit, his former leading lady, was starring on her own and beating him out in the press. She had deserted Macready, wearied of playing second fiddle to the great man. *Punch* had at one time commented that they supposed "Mr. Macready thought Miss Helen Faucit had a very handsome back, for, when on the stage with her, he always managed that the audience should see it and little else."

In the spring of 1845 Macready was having difficulties even with his friends. "Forster spoke to me at dinner in so rude a manner, so grossly impertinent, telling me my opinions were 'unworthy of me,' etc., that Dickens expected I should reply very angrily to him, and White was surprised at his tone and language. He forgets himself." Repeatedly he found Forster

MR. MACREADY AS HAMLET

MR. STUART AS THE GHOST

"not agreeable," and trying "to re-establish a better understanding." Even Bulwer-Lytton, Macready found trying to
"serve himself" under pretext of "serving me," and stooping
to "mingling the trader with the friend." But what was still
more surprising, in the light of earlier and later tirades to the
contrary, Macready was finding British high society unpal-
atable. "I cannot feel with this aristocracy—I dislike it, 'and
something more.'" He was getting "more and more dis-
gusted with the aristocracy and the aristocratic spirit of this
country." At one point during Forrest's engagement he got
so low that he found himself "wishing [to be] in America."
All in all, it was an unhappy season for Macready.

Forrest, unable to arrange any performances in Paris and
unwilling to face the unfriendliness of London audiences,
decided to try the provinces. Away from the city he found
warmhearted applause and genuine friendliness. There had
been no attempt to undermine his out-of-town engagements,
if indeed such would have been possible. The provincial
audiences had never been particularly friendly toward Macready, and he had often spoken of how "disgusting, vulgar,
ignorant, and noisy" they were and of their inability to appreciate a genuine actor. With their low tastes they preferred
the undisciplined blustering of Mr. and Mrs. Charles Kean
or of Edwin Forrest.

The audiences in Cork, Belfast, Dublin, Manchester, and
Sheffield delighted in Forrest's full-bodied and expansive
performances. In Sheffield he was presented with a silver
snuffbox inscribed, "Presented to Edwin Forrest, Esq., by
the members of the Sheffield Theatrical Company, as a mark
of their esteem for him as an ACTOR and a MAN." The
presentation speech was delivered by Gustavus V. Brooke,
an actor whom Macready had found "distressingly bad."
Brooke praised Forrest's wonderful talents and his courteous

behavior to his fellow players. The American actor responded with humble thanks. There could be no greater honor, he said, than to be "praised by one's fellow workers," and what was more important, in view of his experiences in London, "these courtesies shown to one another are productive of a vast amount of good." Outside London Forrest received the kind of cheering reception to which he was accustomed. If he had been depressed with his misfortunes in the capital, the enthusiasm of the provincial audiences had restored his confidence.

His spirits were running high when, on March 2, 1846, he took a night off to have a look at the activities of his competitor. This was at the Theatre Royal in Edinburgh.

Macready had closed his engagement at the Princess in London with *Richelieu* on the night of February 27, and now, the day before his fifty-third birthday, he was in Edinburgh to play *Hamlet*. Macready may have been prepared for an unfriendly audience—he had once said of Edinburgh, "I do not know that if I could afford to do without it I should ever wish to act there again." But he was certainly not prepared to present his talents for Forrest's inspection. Indeed, his immediate report to his diary indicated that he was not aware of Forrest's presence. "On reviewing the performance I can conscientiously pronounce it one of the very best I have given of Hamlet. At the waving of the handkerchief before the play [i.e., the player's scene] and 'I must be idle,' a man on the right side of the stage—upper boxes or gallery, but said to be upper boxes—hissed! The audience took it up, and I waved the more, and bowed derisively and contemptuously to the individual. The audience carried it, though he was very staunch to his purpose. It discomposed me, and alas! might have ruined many; but I bore it down. I thought of speaking to the audience, if called on, and spoke to Murray about it, but he very discreetly dissuaded me. Was called for, and very warmly greeted."

Macready no doubt had forgotten his previous diary note on the parliamentary orator who had subdued such a response with the admonition, "You may hiss, but you cannot sting!" Or was the phrase inappropriate? This hiss had stung, and the sting went deeper as it became apparent that Forrest was the hisser. At first it was attributed to a "Mr. W——," who was in company with Forrest, but when Murray, the theatre manager, and John Ryder (at this time Macready's personal manager) seemed to be so "possessed with the belief," Macready, with seeming reluctance, wrote, "I begin to think he [Forrest] was the man." Then a Mr. Smibert and a Mr. Aitken, who professed to be in the box with Forrest, came forward to say they *"saw him* hiss." The final evidence was supplied by the police. The officer on duty, who was obliged to record all unusual occurrences at the theatre, had entered Forrest's name on the "blotter" as the originator of the disturbance. Two days later, with the aloofness that Macready could summon on such occasions, he reported to his diary: "Indeed, it seems placed beyond all doubt. I feel glad that it is not an Englishman—but no Englishman would have done a thing so base; indeed he *dared* not have done it, and that was one argument in my mind for my belief in Mr. Forrest's guilt. I do not think that such an action has its parallel in all theatrical history! The low-minded ruffian! That man would commit a murder, if he dare." At the moment Macready found no one in Edinburgh rallying to his support. The above entry, coming two days after the incident, continued, "Acted King Lear, to a very middling house (they will not come to see me here)

which was cold in the extreme; there were a few persons
that seemed to understand me, but it is a slaughterous work
to act these characters to these audiences."

Forrest's famous hiss was the shot that declared open war
between the two actors. Macready could never forget nor
forgive such conduct.

Nearly two years later, in 1848, when Macready was in the
U. S. gathering together his "white-papers," he sought all
the firsthand testimony that he could get from sources in
Edinburgh and persuaded Ryder to appear before a justice
of the peace in Chatham County, Georgia. Ryder swore to
the following affidavit: "Before me, Edward D. Wilson, a
Justice of the Peace in and for the County and State aforesaid,
personally appeared John Ryder, who, being duly sworn
deposeth and saith, that Mr. Edwin Forrest (and Mr. Edwin
Forrest only) did hiss Mr. William Charles Macready in the
Theatre Royal, Edinburgh, in the character of Hamlet on
the night of Monday, March 2d, 1846, and that there was not
one single hiss from any other person through that evening."
W. H. Murray, manager of the Theatre Royal, wrote to
Macready on December 28, 1848: "On the evening when Mr.
Forrest hissed Mr. Macready, it was stated to the latter gentleman in the green-room of the Theatre Royal, Edinburgh,
that Mr. Forrest had done so; to which Mr. Macready replied,
'I cannot believe it, Mr. Forrest is too much the gentleman
to adopt such conduct.' This was said in my hearing, and I
feel it but justice to Mr. Macready to state it." The clincher
was provided by the High Sheriff of Edinburgh, Mr. Gordon, in his letter of December 16, 1848. His three-page es-
pousal of Macready's cause described the fateful night in
these words: "The audience was perfectly tranquil, and
breathlessly silent, at the moment Forrest alone hissed. You

know *how silent* an Edinburgh audience can be. [Macready knew.] When that hiss was heard, there was an outbreak by the audience for a moment to put down the person whoever he was, whose sibilation so marred the universal feeling of the house. Not one human being hissed Macready on that night except Forrest." Gordon's final and unequivocal judgment was squeezed into his final sentence. "Believe me, there was but one hiss—and one hisser. Forrest was the hisser— Forrest's was the hiss."

Still another account of the episode is given by John Coleman, the English actor-manager, who was playing Marcellus in Macready's company. "Macready had acquired various tricks, one of which was to strut from side to side just before the play scene, extravagantly flirting his handkerchief above his head [an odd bit of stage business that was later described by Forrest as the *pas de mouchoir*] and behaving less like Hamlet than Osric. On this Edinburgh night, when he knew himself to be acting with particular power and discrimination and the audience was cordially with him, he came to the line 'I must be idle.' As he spoke, he waved the handkerchief, and from the upper boxes on the right-hand side of the stage, there issued a long, sustained hiss like the sound of a steam engine." Coleman reported that he looked up and recognized the man immediately, "his square brow, noble head, dark eyes, blue-black beard, bulldog jaw above a turned-down white collar, and arms folded on his broad chest. It was Edwin Forrest, looking as he had in *The Gladiator* when he said, 'Let them come; we are prepared.' "

Why Macready sought so desperately to incriminate Forrest, who had never made any attempt to conceal his role in the affair, is, on the face of it, rather hard to understand. As

early as March, 1846, Forrest had outlined his views on the
Edinburgh incident in a letter to the London *Times*:

There are two legitimate modes of evincing approbation and
disapprobation in the theatre,—one expressive of approval, by
the clapping of hands, and the other by hisses to mark dissent;
and, as well-timed and hearty applause is the just meed of the
actor who deserves well, so also is hissing a salutary and wholesome corrective of the abuses of the stage; and it was against one
of these abuses that *my* dissent was expressed, and not, as it was
stated, "with a view of expressing his (my) disapproval of the
manner in which Mr. Macready gave effect to a particular passage." The truth is, Mr. Macready thought fit to introduce a fancy
dance into his performance of "Hamlet," which I thought, and
still think, a desecration of the scene, and at which I evinced that
disapprobation, for which the pseudo-critic [in the *Scotsman*] is
pleased to term me an "offender"; and this was the only time during the performance that I did so, . . . The writer of the article in
the *Scotsman,* who has most unwarrantably singled me out for
public animadversion, has carefully omitted to notice the fact
that I warmly applauded several points of Mr. Macready's performance; and more than once I regretted that the audience did
not second me in so doing.

Coleman's description of Macready's eccentric getup for
Hamlet is also of interest: "He wore a dress, the waist of
which nearly reached his arms; a hat with a sable plume big
enough to cover a hearse; a pair of black silk gloves, much
too large for him; a ballet shirt of straw-coloured satin,
which looked simply dirty; and, what with his gaunt, awkward, angular figure, his grizzled hair, his dark beard close
shaven to his square jaws, yet unsoftened by a trace of pig-
ment, his irregular features, his queer, extraordinary nose—
unlike anything else in the shape of a nose I have ever seen—
and his long skinny neck, he appeared positively hideous."
The contrast with Forrest's rugged appearance and muscular

style of acting is underlined by the description written by
one London reviewer who declared that Forrest had "shot
up like the wild mountain pine and prairie sycamore, amid
the free life and spontaneous growths of the west, not rolled
in the garden-bed of cities to a dead level, nor clipped of all
proportion by too careful husbandry." The difference in tem-
peraments was absolute; Forrest could not have been expected to have much patience with his rival's interpretation
of Shakespeare.

Macready fulfilled his Edinburgh engagement in sadness
and fear. On the ninth of March, 1846, he reported that he
"felt rather nervous and uneasy from the uncertainty whether this American ruffian may not have left some colleague
or hireling here instructed to renew the insulting outrage on
me. Reasoned against it, but it is scarcely possible to acquire
full confidence—indispensable to acting—under such an apprehension of doubt." He was completely unstrung and dis-
illusioned. "These people [the Edinburgh audiences] can see
genius in all the harlequin quackeries, devoid of a glimpse
of idea, of Mr. C. Kean, and inspiration in the rant of Miss
Helen Faucit, to which the houses are crowded. But I am not
one of the Edinburgh wonders. . . . Edinburgh is lost to me
as a place of income, a circumstance very much to be regretted by myself, and one I have striven against, unavailing-
ly it seems; I have not talent, or the people have not taste to
appreciate me, it is of little moment now which; my life is
near its close—I will not go on."

And the unfortunate episode in Edinburgh had occurred
at a moment when his disappointment in the British aristocracy was leading him toward a more sympathetic regard
for American democracy. Now he was obliged, in all right-
eousness, to reverse himself. "I feel I cannot *stomach* the
United States as a nation; the good there, I must admit,

appears like the quantity of the grains of wheat to the bushel
of chaff. . . . No more of America for me!"

When Macready returned to London, in April, 1846, and
Forster showed him Forrest's letter in the *Times,* he was by
then sufficiently composed to adopt his normal tone of ironic
magnanimity. "This seems to me (though, of course, offensive, as anything filthy in the physical or material world
would be) to be the seal of his character. Here stands self-
confessed this citizen of the United States, to whom the
greatest harm that I can do, I will: which is to give him the
full benefit of his noble, tasteful, and critical qualities, and
'leave him alone with his glory.' "

Forrest, after completing his engagements in the provinces,
came back to London in time to officiate at an Independence
Day celebration at the Lyceum Tavern, and in August, 1846,
sailed for the United States. Again the two actors drew away
before a showdown, but the Edinburgh hiss had planted the
seeds of mutual hostility and had left Macready feeling
morbid and dejected. In the future there could be little hope
for even a superficial show of professional courtesy between
Forrest and Macready.

A Card for a Card

CHAPTER FIVE ★ ★ ★

Forrest's American friends, knowing of his frustrations in Europe, prepared to give him a rousing welcome when he reappeared at the Park as Lear on September 14, 1846. And as if to comfort him for what might have been regarded as a wasted season in England, the critics assured him that his playing had now acquired a "dignified repose" and a "tone wholly unlike the unrepressed energy and overwhelming physical power that formerly characterized his style."

After his first performance Forrest appeared before the curtain to state his position in regard to Macready. Above

MACREADY AS IAGO

all things he wanted only "to bring the American stage within the influence of a progressive movement." He did not hold any "ungenerous motives toward the really deserving of any other country." The immediate cheers were supported with the proposal of a banquet celebration to honor the recently returned hero. On October 10, a formalized invitation was delivered to Forrest bearing the names of forty-four prominent citizens. Among them were William Cullen Bryant, Parke Godwin, Fitz-Greene Halleck, Prosper M. Wetmore, Evert Duyckinck, and Theodore Sedgwick. Forrest specified the sixteenth as the date for the testimonial occasion. Bryant presided and introduced the guest of honor, applauding his generosity toward his rivals by preserving "the magnanimous silence of conscious greatness." Forrest thanked Bryant for his gracious praise but begged his leave to break that "magnaminous silence" for a moment: "Even before I had appeared, I was threatened with critical castigation, and some of the very journals which, upon my former appearance in London, applauded me to the echo, now assailed me with bitterest denunciations. Criticism was degraded from its high office." But, he was happy to report, sober judgment had finally won out over the "hireling scribblers" and the "theatrical cliques." He and his fellow American actors could prove themselves in "successful comparison with any of the 'stars' that twinkle on us from abroad." What pleased him most in being back on friendly ground was that he could now proceed with his energetic encouragement of our new "National Drama." The sweet harmony of the occasion convinced Forrest that he could assume the perquisites of the "first" actor on the American stage. A prophet with honor in his own country, he could now command the same terms, half the box-office gross, as Macready had drawn from the reluctant American managers.

When Macready saw a newspaper account of Forrest's triumphant reception and the eulogy to his "professional excellence and private worth!!" his diary boiled over with exclamation marks and underscorings. "America!! Give me a crust in England. God speed me in my labours for my blessed family's sake. Amen! No *America*." The United States was a "country for blackguards." But even as he insisted that gentlemen were "certainly the *very* small minority!" he unhappily discovered the names of Bryant, Halleck, and Sedgwick among those on the Forrest banquet committee. Three months later, however, Macready was again speculating on going to America. "I do not like it, but must make the best of it, if we cannot live here." Throughout the next year and a half he was wavering back and forth. At one time he found the "American nation a humbug and a cheat." He could not "go among those ——!" But by April, 1848, he was becoming resigned to the idea of leaving England again: "I deliberated, measured, calculated, but my investigation only served to strengthen the belief that to live and educate my children I must go to the United States. Forster came to dine; he combated very earnestly my arguments, but I am not convinced that he is right, though 'in my heart something battles on his side.'"

Macready's audiences had been falling off, and he had been plagued again by the sort of unhappy incidents that were brought on by his outbursts of temperament. Purportedly Macready had struck an actor's wife on the head "so hard that she was near fainting on the stage." A supernumerary named Richardson received compensation of three pounds from Macready's lawyers for the indignity of having his ear pulled. Repeatedly the diary recorded his "uneasy nights" resulting from his differences with Mr. Maddox, manager of the Princess Theatre, and his annoyance with the "conceited and ignorant persons" who called themselves players. The wine cup became so necessary to bolster his performances that he recorded with self-righteous pleasure the occasions when he managed to play without stimulants.

Relief had to be secured somehow, even if in America. By the middle of the summer, 1848, against the advice of his intimates and against his own better judgment, he had made up his mind to cross the Atlantic again. Perceiving his determination, a small group of friends urged the Drury Lane management to schedule a Macready benefit, but even this did not turn out well. Throughout most of his life Macready had condemned the low-life character and boorish manners of his colleagues in the acting profession. It seems never to have occurred to him that these abused inferiors might bear some ill feeling toward him. This they most assuredly did. Mrs. Hunt, later Mrs. John Drew, expressed the sentiments of many when she wrote, "Macready was a dreadful man to act with; you had the unpleasant sensation of knowing that you were doing nothing that he wanted you to, though following strictly his instructions. He would press you down with his hand on your head, and tell you in an undertone to stand up!" George Vandenhoff, another actor who had performed with Macready, wrote of the master's upstaging technique. "Authors were lopped and pared down in speeches that did not belong to *him;* and actors were expected and compelled to lose all thought of giving prominence to their own parts, when he was on the stage." His part must be *"the* feature of the play. When he played Othello, Iago was to be *nowhere!* Othello was to be the *sole* consideration. Iago was a mere *stoker* whose business it was to supply Othello's passion with fuel. The next night, perhaps, he took Iago and lo! presto! everything was changed. Othello was to become a mere puppet for Iago to play with.

Othello was to be a mere fly, a large *blue-bottle,* struggling in the meshes of the Italian spider."

On the occasion of the Drury Lane benefit, which was announced for July 10, this brooding resentment against Macready rose to the surface. Placards appeared about London asking, "Who acts for Mr. Macready?"—taunting him with the "Mr." (He always insisted on being addressed as William C. Macready, Esq.) But in spite of the opposition a company was finally engaged. Macready, alert to the possibility of further disturbances in the theatre, commissioned Charles Dickens, his manager for the night, and Forster to see that "seven or eight policemen in plain clothes" were distributed about the pit. In spite of the police and the presence of the Queen and her royal party, an organized commotion in the pit and gallery began as soon as the curtain went up. During the second scene—the play was *Henry VIII* —Macready requested permission of the Queen to address the audience. With her leave, he spoke to the pit and gallery: "Happy as I have been in receiving favours from them for many years, they would now add to my obligations by receiving their money and leaving the theatre." Enough of them departed at this invitation—collecting ninety pounds in refunds—to allow the play to proceed in comparative quiet, and Macready was given an enthusiastic "call" at the end of his performance. Obviously this was not a full-audience protest against Macready—there were some £1,100 left in the till after the refunds had been paid—but the occasion was certainly not a triumph for him.

Sailing for America on September 9, 1848, he was still filled with misgivings about the wisdom of his decision. Forrest, he knew, would be hostile to the invasion, but Macready had also received "insinuations that Miss Cushman was endeavoring to do [him] mischief in America." His old friend Charles Dickens, whom he had expected to see on board, sent a letter of regrets, a letter which, though apologetic, encouraged still more fear and apprehension. Dickens wrote in part: "I have lately had grave doubts of the propriety of my seeing you on board the steamer. It will be crowded with Americans at this season of the year and, believe me, they are not the people you suppose them to be. So strongly have I felt that my accompanying you on board would be, after the last *Chuzzlewit,* fatal to your success and certain to bring down upon you every species of insult and outrage, that I have all along determined within myself to remain in the hotel and charge the landlord to keep my being there a secret."

With these thoughts to brood on for thirteen days, Macready was prepared for a cool, if not openly hostile, reception; and it was probably more Dickens' warnings combined with his own misgivings than any firsthand observations that provoked his morose diary entry of September 26, the first after his arrival in Boston. "I come here with a most affectionate feeling towards many friends, with a preference for the form of government established, and with a *wish,* a strong wish to make a home here for myself and my beloved children. *But* the low standard of taste, the ruffianly tone of the class immediately below *the best,* . . . shock and in truth disgust me. The complacency, indeed the *approbation* with which a paper speaks of the '*independence*' of Mr. Forrest (an ignorant, uneducated man, burning with envy and rancour at my success) hissing me in the Edinburgh Theatre, makes me feel that I seek in vain to accommodate myself to such utterly uncongenial natures. I fear it is not *possible* to live here, but that a cottage and seclusion—(alas! alas! for my dear, dear girls!)—is the prospect of my declining years; to me *alone* sufficient for happiness, but for *them,* with life

before them, how *triste* and gloomy!" Macready delivered
himself of this elaborate meditation only two days after arriving at Boston, but it is probable that a single newspaper
item mentioning Forrest had infected the whole atmosphere.
At the very moment when Macready arrived, Forrest was
just winding up a run of twenty-three consecutive nights as
the star attraction at the Broadway Theatre in New York.

In the interval between the fall of 1846, when Forrest returned to New York, and the fall of 1848, when Macready reinvaded American theatrical territory, Forrest had
stormed around the country affirming his position as the
foremost American actor and accumulating a fortune. He
realized that the fruit of an actor's labors must be sold at
the maximum price during the brief period of his full ma-
turity. Wherever he went—Cincinnati, Louisville, Philadelphia, New Orleans, Mobile—he bargained for a straight $200
a night or half the gross. His terms seem to have been as-
tutely arranged. In Louisville, where he signed for $200, the
manager was obliged on a couple of occasions to add $50 of
his own to the box-office receipts to make up Forrest's fee.
In New Orleans, where Forrest chose half the gross for an
engagement of thirty nights, his share averaged $257 a night.
Only in St. Louis was he unable to come to terms. Sol Smith,
probably the sharpest of the Western managers, would accede to neither arrangement; and Forrest, who stuck to his
demands, missed St. Louis. During the spring and summer
of 1848, after a season in New York, Forrest made another
tour of the South and West, playing in Chicago, Detroit,
and Buffalo on his way back to New York. On August 28,
he began the Broadway engagement that was still in progress when Macready landed in Boston.

These were unmistakably triumphant seasons for Forrest, even though the houses were not always crowded to

MACREADY AS SHYLOCK

capacity and the critics not invariably galvanized by his emotional prowess. The New York *Courier and Enquirer* (March 30, 1847) found "his whole style rough, unrefined, heavy, and laborious. His gentlemen are not such as Shakespeare drew; they are great roaring boys that cry like fat babies, and puff and blow like sledge men." This critic objected particularly to the death scenes: "How they die! The actor staggers in all gory, breathing so that the gods may hear; he falls, gasps, the blood gets in his throat, he strangles—faugh!" Nevertheless, although some genteel souls may have objected to these exertions, they were exactly what endeared Forrest to the mass of his followers and certified his genius. In the eyes of his countrymen he was a truly heroic American actor.

Macready had gotten safely on shore in the fall of 1848, but he held, if he held at all, a very uncertain beach head in Boston. There was no doubt as to who held the mainland. Forrest was at the height of his popularity; Macready was a dejected, displaced English actor whose fortunes were in need of repair. His mood was evidently reflected in his appearance and manner, which were briefly noted by Longfellow. In his journal entry of September 25, 1848, Longfellow wrote, "Dined with Felton, to meet Macready, who looks rather pale and ill and comes with long ear-locks."

Although his position decreed a certain humility, Macready was incapable of being humble. Instead of opening his American invasion with an appearance in Boston, he moved directly on to New York to offer battle in Forrest's stronghold. His engagement began at the Astor Place Opera House on October 4 with a performance of *Macbeth* before a warm and courteous audience—markedly unlike the raging mob that was to greet his final *Macbeth* the following spring. Macready paid tribute to the good taste of the opening night

audience with a curtain speech in which, according to one
newspaper, he spoke of the "present assemblage" as being
the "best refutation of the calumnies of those who had asserted that he was too old and effete to embody the creations
of the great dramatist." This remark was, of course, directed
at Forrest, who had suggested that the English actor should
retire instead of continuing to hobble about the stage. Age
was an obsession with Macready; such a personal matter
should not be spoken of by others, above all not by his ene-
mies. Again and again in the diary, beginning as early as
1844, Macready had worried about "being far advanced in
life." After a bad performance, his first question was always,
"Am I growing old?"

Macready played through his Shakespearean repertoire in
ten performances, closing with a benefit performance (for
Macready's benefit) of *The Merchant of Venice* on October
25. During these three weeks he was never free of the apprehension that a "project was on foot to excite a hostile feeling
against him with the American public." On the twelfth he
reported that he "acted Hamlet, not without some uncertainty as to whether some friends of Forrest might not be in
the theatre on purpose to give colour by their disapprobation
to the 'justice' of his outrageous conduct in hissing me." In
fact, every diary entry for this period makes some scornful
yet fearful reference to his antagonist. And even before the
end of his New York stay, Macready had concluded that
America was no place for him. On the sixteenth he wrote,
"This evening has decided me. In this country, the masses,
rich and poor, are essentially ignorant and vulgar—utterly
deficient in taste and without the modesty to distrust themselves. A crust in England is better than pampering tables
here. *'I am for England—*God!'"

Although there was no overt interference with Macready's

FORREST AS MACBETH

New York engagement, his presence did not pass unnoticed by his detractors. The theatrical producers who specialized in topical burlesques, a favorite form of nineteenth-century American theatre, found Macready a stimulating subject. *Who's Got Macready? or, a Race to Boston* (the principal characters were Mr. Park, Mr. Broadway, and Mr. Astorplace) opened at the Olympic on October 6, and *Mr. Macgreedy, or, a Star at the Opera House* ran for two weeks, beginning October 9, at the National Theatre. The first of these was undoubtedly directed at some of Macready's difficulties in arranging his New York engagement. He had wished to appear at the National, but Mr. Pelby, the manager, had refused to accede "to the dictatorial terms of this actor autocrat." These satires, running concurrently with Macready's performances, must have galled him.

He was probably glad to get away from New York to try his luck in Boston. At least in Boston—where he dined with William Prescott, George T. Curtis, Charles Eliot Norton, and George Ticknor—Macready had a society of people of "taste" who were to his taste; but even the soothing assurances of these literary bigwigs were inadequate to balance the public unfriendliness that greeted him. On the morning of October 30 (he was to open that night at the Howard Athenaeum) he was welcomed with a defamatory piece in the Boston *Mail* under the comprehensive heading: "More about McReady [*sic*]—His Abuse of Forrest in Europe—Endeavors to put him down in Paris, London, and Edinburgh—His Intrigue with Bulwer to prevent Forrest playing Bulwer's pieces—His Abuse of Americans." All the stops were pulled. The story began, "Mr. McReady has at length arrived, and next to the grand water celebration will create such excitement, as will emphatically mark the present epoch in time's calendar. He plays this evening at the Howard Athenaeum, and refuses to show himself for less than one dollar a ticket." But what was the real objection to Macready? "Has he not the same right as other men have, to do as he pleases?" the writer asked, and then answered:

He has a right to come to this country in the exercise of his profession; he has a right to demand a dollar from every person who witnesses his acting, and if managers of Theatres are willing to accede to his arbitrary proposals, he has certainly a right to make them. We complain not of any of these. Our charges against McReady are based upon more important grounds. It is *his conduct in his own country in relation to Mr. Forrest, that we are about investigating; his inhospitality, his crushing influence, his vindictive opposition, and his steadfast determination to ruin the prospects of that gentleman in England, that we bring to his door.* Let him deny them if he can.

With his friends in Boston ready to relieve the oppressiveness of unsympathetic audiences, Macready might have kept his composure if he had found his colleagues on the stage more to his liking. But, according to his diary, he was forced to act with "a Desdemona of 50, patched up to 45, . . . a Catherine and a Mrs. Oakley to make a dog vomit!" And he attempted *Lear* "with a Goneril—perhaps sober, but acting the distressful!—with a Cordelia talking nonsense, haggard and old as Tisiphone, and affecting the timid; a Fool singing *horribly out of tune,* but by far the best of the bunch; that great loud, Mr. Ryder, as bad as the worst of them. I acted *against* it all, striving to keep my self-possession, and I acted *well.* The curtain fell, and the audience, who would have cheered on a thick-headed, thick-legged *brute* like Mr. Forrest, took no notice of this, my best performance. This is the civilization—the growing *taste* of the United States!!!"

The villainous image of Forrest was inescapable. When Macready quit his brief Boston engagement and moved on

to Philadelphia, he encountered Forrest on the street the first
day there. "Forrest bowed to Gould, who saluted him; but
I did not look towards him. I had been telling Gould before
that I should not speak to him if I saw him, and that I should
decline any offer to meet him, as that would be to acquit him
of the unworthy and ungentlemanlike conduct he has displayed to me." This was on November 18, 1848.

On the twentieth Macready was scheduled to open at the
Arch Street Theatre, in Philadelphia. Again, as in Boston,
his presence was noted in the press, but the *Public Ledger*
was more restrained than the Boston *Mail*. "This evening
commences a week of theatrical rivalry.... Macready has to
contend with age. Forrest is in the prime of a vigorous and
robust manhood. Each appears this evening in the character
of Macbeth. The public are not like newspaper folks, gifted
with ubiquity, and those who go to see the one must forego
the pleasure of seeing the other, consequently the public will
be as much divided in opinion as ever." These were kind
words compared with Boston. Even the reference to his age,
a mere fifty-six, did not insinuate that he had lost the battle
with his advancing years.

According to the *Public Ledger* account on the next day,
both Macbeths had done well at the box office. "Forrest had
an immense audience, every part of the theatre, even to the
outside of the box down, being crowded. He went through
his part with unusual spirit and effect, and was warmly applauded." "Macready drew a very crowded audience. The
house inside was packed and outside there was a gathering
large enough for a town meeting." But Macready did not
make out so well with his audience. Several times during
the evening there were cheers for Forrest, and eggs and pennies were thrown to the stage.

Macready, who had been informed that there might be a

disturbance, gave a full account of the occasion in his diary:

I would take no stimulant; had fortunately eaten a light dinner, conscious of having done nothing even questionable. I was prepared. I heard great shouting at Mr. Ryder, who was evidently mistaken by the deputed rioters for myself. Went on, and applause, with the hissing, coarse noises, etc., of the ruffians there, attended my entry. I went through cheerily and defyingly, pointing at the scoundrels such passages as "I dare do all," etc. A rotten egg was thrown on the stage. I went in active and cheerful defiance through it, though injured in the more touching and delicate effects, and in the last scene threw all my heart into the contest, and wound up with great effect.

After the play,

I stood to be heard, and that for a long time, touched and moved at first by the genial and generous warmth of the bulk of the audience. Obtaining at last silence, . . . I observed that, in my country it was an invariable principle of justice not to condemn a man unheard, and that their laws were similar to our own.

Another account, not Macready's, says that there was a voice from the audience at this point: "Did you allow Forrest to be heard in England?" Macready ignored the interruption, but the question was relevant to his matter:

There had been an impression widely and most industriously disseminated that I had shown hostility in my own country to an American actor. I declare upon my 'sacred honour' that, not only were the assertions so made false in the aggregate, but that in all the circumstances carefully compiled there was not for a single one the smallest shadow of foundation. That I had been hissed in a public theatre by an American actor, an act which I believed no other American would have committed, and which I was certain no European actor would have been guilty of. That up to that period I had shown none but kindly feelings towards that person, and had never since then publicly expressed an unkind one. I begged to observe that I was perfectly ready if they desired to relinquish my engagement from that night (*No, No, No!*); and that, under any circumstances, I should recollect with satisfaction and pride the support they had so cordially rendered. Again and again I thanked them and retired. The applause was most fervent.

The speech—and the audience's reaction to it—warmed Macready's spirits. Such gracious magnanimity could not go unrewarded. Colonel Lee, who held the office of recorder in Philadelphia, came backstage, gave him a cigar, and then walked with Macready to his hotel. After tea and some more cigars, Macready retired, unaware that his remarks would be taken as a red flag waving the American bull into the arena.

The *Public Ledger* for November 22, 1848, carried a "card" with Forrest's reply to Macready's opening night remarks.

Mr. Macready in his speech last night to the audience assembled at the Arch Street Theatre, made allusion, I understand, to "an American actor" who had the temerity on one occasion openly to hiss him! This is true, and, by the way, the only truth which I have been enabled to gather from the whole scope of his address. But why say "an American actor?" Why not openly charge me with the act? for I did it, and publicly avowed it in the *Times* newspaper of London, and at the same time asserted my right to do so.

On the occasion alluded to Mr. Macready introduced a fancy dance into his performance of *Hamlet,* which I designated as a *pas de mouchoir,* and which I hissed, for I thought it a desecration of the scene, and the audience thought so, too for in a few nights afterwards, when Mr. Macready repeated the part of Hamlet with the same tomfoolery, the intelligent audience of Edinburgh greeted it with a universal hiss. Mr. Macready is stated to have said last night that up to the time of this act on my part he had never entertained toward me a feeling of unkindness! I unhesitatingly pronounce this to be a wilful and unblushing falsehood. I most solemnly aver and do believe that Mr. Macready, instigated by his narrow, envious mind, and his selfish fears, did secretly—not openly—suborn several writers for the English press to write me down. . . .

I assert, also, and solemnly believe, that Mr. Macready connived, when his friends went to the theatre in London, to hiss me, with the purpose of driving me from the stage, and all this happened many months before the affair at Edinburgh, to which Macready refers, and in relation to which he jesuitically remarks that, 'until that act, he never entertained toward me a feeling of unkindness.' Pah! Mr. Macready has no feeling of kindness for any actor who is likely by his talent to stand in his way. . . . Many of my friends called upon me when Mr. Macready was announced to perform, and proposed to drive him from the stage for his conduct toward me in London. My advice was, do nothing; let the superannuated driveller alone; to oppose him would be but to make him of some importance. . . .

Forrest pricked at Macready's tenderest nerve endings almost as if he had an inner knowledge of the English actor's suffering conscience. His troublesome dealings with other actors, the impression of self-conceit that he created, his concern about his advancing years—these had been Macready's unhappy preoccupations for years; and here was his rival spreading them out for public investigation. On November 22 Macready replied with his own "card to the public" from the Jones Hotel. This was distributed with the theatre programs at the Arch Street Theatre that evening.

In a card published in the *Public Ledger* and other morning papers of this city, Mr. Forrest having avowed himself the author of the statement, which Mr. Macready has solemnly pledged his honor to be without the least foundation, Mr. Macready cannot be wanting in self-respect so far as to bandy words upon the subject; but as the circulation of such statements is manifestly calculated to prejudice Mr. Macready in the opinion of the American

public, and to affect both his professional interests and his estimation in society. Mr. Macready respectfully requests the public to
suspend their judgment upon the questions until the decision of a
legal tribunal, before which he will immediately take measures
to bring it, and before which he will prove his veracity, hitherto
unquestioned, shall place the truth beyond doubt.

His confidence in his own ability to carry on the fight
was rapidly disappearing. He seemed to be in disfavor with
the public, the press, and even his old friends, and he was
depressed by "the ungentlemanly apathy and indifference of
those persons whom I have known here. . . . Not one to call
upon me." Oh, for "a crust in England—a pot of herbs—
rather than luxury with this populace, this nation of ———."

But if Macready despaired of ever finding a kindly audience in America, the public delighted in the sparring of the
two tragedians, whose nightly antics were evidently a source
of more fun than solemnity. On November 23, 1848, the
following paragraph, headed "Actor's Quarrels," appeared
in the *Public Ledger:* "The public are getting into a very
pleasant state of excitement respecting the quarrels of two
distinguished actors at rival theatres, and have got up a
scene or two, not down in the bills, by interfering in an
affair that seems to be merely personal. Really this theatrical
émeute is the most laughable affair that has recently happened. The two great thespian rivals making speeches and
shooting paper pellets at each other's scenes in the form of
cards, remarkable only for exceeding bad temper and coarse
language. Somebody should dramatize this great feud immediately." Even the merchants of the city found in the quarrel
a suitable excuse for advertising. According to one advertisement, printed on November 23, there was "Great excitement
at the Arch Street Theatre, but not less at the Philadelphia
Wardrobe, No. 105 Chestnut Street."

Macready's opinion to the contrary, the press at this time did more to temper and reduce the quarrel to its proper level than it did to fan the rivalry. On December 1, a week before Macready left Philadelphia, an editorial in the *Public Ledger* commented very sensibly on the whole proceedings: "As the quarrels of artists are as common, as habitual, as necessary, as much in course, as the quarrels of children, the public shows deplorable deficiency of good sense and dignity in participating in them. Public pays to see Hamlet *et al*. They do not wish to be 'fobbed off' with Mister Macready and Mister Forrest, who have no business there. People visit the theatre to witness a counterfeit combat between Athenians and Spartans and not a real 'knock-down and drag-out' between 'killers' and 'bouncers!' "

But none of this sanity impressed Macready—or Forrest. Forrest continued his taunts, and Macready grieved to his diary about his mistreatment. "Baited into a petty frenzy," he was willing to quit America even without the prospect of a "crust" in England. "Let me once get *from* this country and give me a dungeon or a hovel in any other, so I be free from this." When some presumptuous critic suggested that Macready should not be dealt with too harshly for he was indeed the "second living actor," Macready's rage was again released in the pages of his diary. " 'Give me an ounce of civit, good apothecary, to sweeten my imagination,' poisoned with the foetor of this disgusting country." Before he left Philadelphia he even engaged the services of two lawyers, W. B. Reed and George Meredith, to prepare and prosecute a case in his behalf. Macready himself began soliciting from all his friends in England letters that might be used in his defense. Reed finally advised Macready to drop the libel suit against Forrest because it would detain him in America longer than he wished to stay; but Macready, not willing to defer in silence, gathered his "Replies" into a volume which he had published by Stringer and Townsend the following May. Some letters from these "Replies" have already been noted.

Macready closed his Philadelphia engagement on December 1, 1848, with a performance of *Hamlet* and then appeared at the Stuyvesant Institute in New York for two Shakespearean readings on December 5 and 8. From there he went on to Baltimore, Washington, Richmond, Charleston, New Orleans (making a delayed appearance there because of the cholera epidemic), and, finally, Cincinnati, where he opened in *Hamlet* on April 2, 1849. During this interval of four months he was free from the immediate pressure of Forrest's competition, but he was not free from his habitual obsessions: his fading popularity, the incompetence of all other actors, and the low state of American culture. His first diary entry (January 4) of the new year was devoted to a disquisition on mortality prefaced with this unhappy observation: "For the first time I saw in the glass to-day that I really am an old man."

At his opening performance of *Hamlet* in Cincinnati some "ruffian from the left side gallery threw into the middle of the stage the half of the raw carcase [*sic*] of a sheep! . . . . These barbarians, the *canaille*—the brutes! I really despise my audience, and dislike them too."

If Macready had thought that a few months away from the metropolitan areas would make his return to New York a more peaceful experience, the intelligence that reached him in Cincinnati instructed him otherwise. The New York papers were discussing the possibility "of certain friends of mine and this blackguard Forrest making the occasion of my appearance a signal for conflict." In one article he and Forrest were advised to "Go it, my chickens." On the twelfth, still in Cincinnati, Macready received a telegram from Gould informing him that Forrest had been engaged to open at the Broadway on April 23. Macready then surmised that all the newspaper fanfare had been only a "villainous proceeding on Forrest's part to get up excitement in the hope it would draw money to him!!! My God!"

If that were Forrest's purpose, Macready resolved to share in the profits. He arrived in New York on the twenty-seventh and immediately contracted with William Niblo and James H. Hackett for a four weeks' engagement at the Astor Place Opera House to begin on May 7.

The Principals Arrive

When Macready arrived in Boston in the fall of 1848, Forrest was playing a triumphant end-of-summer engagement at the Broadway. This was concluded on September 22, almost two weeks before Macready opened in New York. After Macready had completed his New York showings and was off to Boston, Forrest was back for another week at the Broadway, beginning on November 13 and followed immediately by the concurrent engagements of the two men in Philadelphia. Forrest played in Baltimore in the middle of December, just a few days after Macready had departed for his Southern tour; but instead of pursuing

Macready down the coast, Forrest returned to New York. He was not so preoccupied with Macready as with his own domestic problems. Forrest and his wife were at this time enacting the real-life scenes that were, three years later, to be vividly described in one of the sensational divorce trials of the mid-nineteenth century.

The marital difficulties had started the year before. In 1848 Forrest had been accompanied to Cincinnati by his wife and an actor friend, George W. Jamieson. On May 31, according to Forrest's testimony, he had left the hotel to visit a portrait painter. Not finding the painter at home, he returned to his quarters earlier than expected. "When I entered my private parlor in the City Hotel, I preceded S. S. Smith, who was with me, some yards, and found Mrs. Forrest standing between the knees of Mr. Jamieson, who was sitting on the sofa, with his hands upon her person. I was amazed and confounded, and asked what it meant. Mrs. Forrest replied, with considerable perturbation, that Mr. Jamieson had been pointing out her phrenological developments. Being of an unsuspicious nature, and anxious to believe that it was nothing more than an act of imprudence on her part, I was for a time quieted by this explanation." Such gallant testimony, if unbelievably naïve, certainly demonstrated Forrest's desire to preserve his marriage.

During the season following the Cincinnati incident, all his efforts went in this direction. Whatever time and energy could be spared from his professional engagements he devoted to his projected love nest, "Fonthill Castle," a gray granite structure designed in a mixture of Norman and Gothic and overlooking the Hudson immediately above Riverdale. This romantic edifice was typical of the domestic architecture of that area and symbolized, in the fashion of the time, domestic felicity and financial success. In No-

vember Forrest staged a "roofing" celebration for all the
workmen on the job and was rewarded with sweet praise
from an anonymous orator. "His industry and wealth have
employed you. His perseverance has raised this majestic
monument, a monument that will stand as a beacon-light to
the present and future generations; . . . and the lesson which
every person may learn will be, that as industry, perseverance, frugality, temperance, and genius have raised stone
upon stone, so there is hope for you all." This was the kind
of language Forrest was accustomed to. It was like a speech
from *Metamora*.

Forrest planned, as he said in the "confession of intents"
deposited in the cornerstone, "to build a desirable, spacious
and comfortable abode for myself and my wife, to serve us
during our natural lives, and at our death to endow the
building with sufficient yearly income, so that a certain number of decayed or superannuated actors and actresses of
American birth (*all foreigners* to be strictly excluded) may
inhabit the mansion and enjoy the grounds thereunto belonging, so long as they live." How empty these sentiments
must have seemed six years later, when Forrest was obliged
to sell "Fonthill Castle" to a religious sisterhood. (The
building is now the library of the College of Mount St. Vin-
cent.)

It was not until January, 1849, that Forrest became convinced that he and Catherine would not occupy the romantic
citadel. In December he had written to her from Baltimore,
"I am sitting at an open window, in the Eutaw House; and
while I write, there is above me a clear, blue, cloudless sky—
just such a day as I yearn to have with you at Fonthill."
Early in January he discovered a "love note" from Jamieson
to his wife, and as he unwillingly began to solicit the opinion
of his friends, he learned that there was fairly common talk

that Catherine had, in his absence, maintained "late hours
and easy manners" not only with Jamieson but with Captain
Calcraft and Richard Willis, a brother of the writer and
editor, N. P. Willis. For the next four months Forrest made
a gentlemanly effort to deny the damning evidence, but he
finally gave up.

It is curious to note that George Jamieson, although he
had been the first to arouse Forrest's suspicions, came out as
one of Forrest's champions after the riot in May. Appearing
in Cleveland when the news reached that city, he delivered
a curtain speech to a cheering audience, praising Forrest,
condemning Macready, and praying that "the time would
come when American actors would do the American acting."

On the anniversary of Shakespeare's birthday, April 23,
1849, Forrest opened at the Broadway Theatre in *Othello*.
Five days later he and his wife separated. Forrest escorted
her from their house on Twenty-second Street to the home
of their good friends Mr. and Mrs. Parke Godwin. All was
accomplished with great gentility, if we accept the account
provided by James Lawson in his letter to John Sinclair
(Catherine's father) in London. He wrote on May 1, "From
the time this unhappy affair was concluded on between
them, Mrs. Forrest has conducted herself, as she always does,
with admirable discretion; not a murmur has escaped her
lips. Mr. Forrest has always been kind and considerate, and
nothing in his conduct gives warrant for angry feelings or
unkind treatment. He thinks he has made a self-sacrifice
for some high principle; what, I know not."

The entire document continued in this tone. If Lawson
knew anything of the difficulties, he discreetly withheld
them from Catherine's father. There is no doubt, however,
that Forrest was saddened by the disintegration of his mar-

riage and angered by the unnerving suspicions that precipitated the break. He was in no temper to smile upon any further aggravations to his psychical composure. And it was just at this critical moment that Macready came back to the city to submit a final challenge to the American actor.

Before Macready began his final engagement, Forrest was well into one of the most successful runs of his career. With the exception of a one-night stand in *Macbeth* at the Astor Place Opera House on February 8, 1849, for the benefit of the American Dramatic Fund Association, Forrest had not been seen in New York since the previous November. Deprived of his presence for this long period and aware of the unpleasant rumors relating to his domestic difficulties, his followers were prepared to give him a rousing welcome. A few at least must have been further conditioned by the announcement of Macready's impending arrival in the city, briefly noted in the *Morning Express* of April 23, the day on which Forrest opened at the Broadway in *Othello*. That evening the theatre was crowded to overflowing, "every standing place even being occupied. . . . Of Mr. Forrest's acting it is unnecessary to say much, because it has been criticized so often and so thoroughly as to render any further elaborate notice of it superfluous. Suffice it to say that it was worthy of his great name and fame. . . . At the conclusion of the tragedy, he was called vociferously before the curtain, but he did not speak, he simply bowed his acknowledgements for the honor thus conferred upon him." These comments appeared in the *Herald* the following day.

But the *Herald* did not confine itself to the performance. Another page of the paper carried a letter from Forrest dated April 10. The editors had undoubtedly held it for publication on the newsworthy occasion of Forrest's reappearance at the Broadway, which was nearly simultaneous with the announcement of Macready's imminent return to the city. Forrest wrote in part,

I intended, some days since, to indite this letter, but my time has been much more agreeably employed looking after the affairs of my farm, which at this season of the year, presents to me the most delightful attractions.

I have been given conclusive English authority that a certain clique existed in London to write me down, and that the writer in the *Examiner* was the bell-wether of the flock. I am now happy to furnish you with the testimony of one of our own countrymen, who, from his intercourse with Albany Fonblanque, Esq. [the editor and proprietor of the *Examiner*] and other gentlemen intimately connected with him, had opportunities to know the feelings under which Mr. Forster wrote, and how his feelings were regarded by those who best understood the relation in which Mr. Forster stood to Mr. Macready. You will perceive that Mr. Forster is not the editor of the *Examiner*, but is, as I said in a former letter, the "hireling scribbler" of its theatrical and literary articles.

Forrest next proceeded to quote a letter dated February 9, 1849, which explained in detail "that it was to win the favor of his friend and patron, Mr. Macready, that Forster did his best not only to write down his American rival, but to stir up such opposition as would militate against his (your) success in England. . . . The letter was signed *****, and the asterisks were followed by Forrest's explanation that "I do not deem it necessary to give the name of the writer of this letter, but he is ready, at any moment, should the occasion require it, to make the most solemn attestation to the truth of what he has written."

Forrest then undertook to review some of the misdeeds of his rival: his shabby treatment of Gustavus V. Brooke, the young and talented Irish tragedian, whom Macready at-

tempted to "put on the shelf" because he could not "brook a
rival near his throne"; his insistence on having all the actors
in his company "move and speak according to his teachings
and imitate his absurd mannerisms and peculiarities." Forrest quoted at length from an article in the Edinburgh *Pilot
and Chronicle* of March, 1846, in explaining that the pages
of the *Examiner* had been used to discredit the playing of
Charles Kean when Kean was drawing larger houses in
London than Macready. The success that Miss Faucit had
achieved when she got out from under Macready's thumb
and "unlearned Macready's mannerisms" was also commented on. Forrest was aware that these were all sore points
with Macready, but he was equally aware that Macready
had started soliciting his own documentary evidence in the
previous November.

On Wednesday evening (April 25) Forrest performed
Richelieu before a "crowded audience," and in this "deline-
ation," according to the *Herald,* he "got rid of much of that
burlesque roughness which had disfigured it in his hands
some time ago." On the following evening, his *Macbeth*
was greeted with another "crowded house" and with special
praise from the press for his magnificent costumes and the
music that was inserted into the production. Forrest was indeed riding high. On the twenty-seventh the *Evening Post*
wrote, "The legitimate—it is not dead!—It is not languish-
ing! See the houses that are attracted to the Broadway. The
great house that payed homage to *Macbeth*, most finely
played by the most understanding and most capable of
tragedians, Edwin Forrest."

But the press and the public were even more interested in
the continuing quarrel between Forrest and Macready.
James Gordon Bennett, particularly, saw the possibilities of

toying with Forrest's letter of April 10 in some gay and playful journalese. His *Herald* for April 26 carried a piece under the heading, "FORREST'S FORAY UPON THE MACS."

We have been inundated with correspondence, grave and gay, serious and sarcastic, relative to the curious literary productions with which Mr. Forrest has been recently electrifying or stultifying the public—we hardly know which is the proper epithet to be used on the solemn occasion. The following is the shortest, and we give it:—

My Dear Sir.—I am sure you are very obliging and therefore feel confident you will publish this note. Every few days your always amusing paper is crammed with the literary productions of Mr. Forrest, who by his confession, is thus endeavoring "to define his own position." Do, my dear Mr. Bennett assure him the labor is superfluous and will be more profitably employed on his "farm."

I am, nevertheless, astonished that you, who ordinarily understand the merits of a case so well, should persist, in connection with many of your fellow journalists, in calling Mr. Forrest's affair a quarrel. A quarrel is in one respect, like a bargain—it takes two to make it—and it is as ridiculous to style this a controversy as it would be to place the angel and the sick man at the pool of Bethesda on a footing. The angel troubled the waters, but the sick man was healed thereby. This fact suggests a solution of the enigma that so overtasks Mr. Forrest's brain. He cannot conceive why he should have been unfavorably received by the British critics of the British stage, unless through the agency of one whom he is pleased to call his rival. Now the ill-success, the disease lies in himself, and unless he layes [*sic*] in the agitated waters—that is, catches something of the fine tact, nice conception and studied elegance of his and the drama's master spirit—he may cease to wonder, if the discriminating do not, although the mass may, raise their hands as he passes by. Is not this your opinion, Mr. Bennett? Do speak out, and oblige your present correspondent.

So and So.

We know a thing or two beyond even what our correspondent Mr. So-and-so seems to be acquainted with. On a second perusal of the last letter of Mr. Forrest—(which, by the by, is not to be the last, for as soon as he plants the early potatoes and puts his cabbages into the ground on his farm near the Gothic Castle on the North River, he intends to give another,)—we have fathomed the mystery of that extraordinary difficulty under which Mr. Forrest appears to labor with regard to Mr. Macready. The enigma is solved. Mr. Forrest's "Last" is preceded by an anonymous note addressed to him, giving him the first intimation of the theatrical intrigues in London and Mr. Macready's enmity, under the significant signature of *******. Now what do these ominous asterisks mean? When we read over this note, before we got half through we became satisfied, from our knowledge of the man, and the intrinsic evidence afforded by the note itself, that the writer was no less a personage than Henry Wikoff—the celebrated Chevalier Wikoff—the notorious Wikoff—the Wikoff who trotted Fanny Ellsler throughout the United States, managed her little affairs and appearances, and then got up a quarrel with her when the pair returned to London.—This note is Wikoff all over. We have no doubt, indeed, that the whole of the prejudice which has been created in the mind of Mr. Forrest against Mr. Macready had been planted there at an early day by the officious conversations and flagrant misrepresentations of this same meddlesome Wikoff, who is a perfect adept in the creation of difficulty among friends, and in multiplying quarrels, from which he takes care to keep himself free. . . . We do not believe that Mr. Macready ever had anything to do with those criticisms in the *Examiner*, or any other paper, which provoked the ire of Mr. Forrest. Mr. Macready is a man too much taken up with his

FORREST AS OTHELLO

FORREST AS RICHARD III

own affairs—too fond of his own fame—too vain of himself, if you please, to trouble himself about others as much as Mr. Forrest imagines.

Forrest did not deny that his informant had been Henry Wikoff. Wikoff had been Forrest's companion on his first trip abroad and had been largely responsible for arranging his meeting with the Sinclairs and his marriage to Catherine.

Macready meanwhile had arrived in New York for his engagement at the Opera House. He and his comrade, Mr. Ryder, took "apartments" at the New York Hotel on Broadway between Washington Place and Waverly, a block and a half from the Astor Place Opera House. On April 28, the day after Macready's arrival, the newspapers carried the first advertisements of his approaching engagement: "ASTOR PLACE OPERA HOUSE. The public are respectfully informed that this splendid establishment will be opened for the performance of the English Drama commencing on Monday, 7th May next with the farewell engagement of Mr. Macready being his last performance in the United States." Macready must have liked the tone and style—no prices (actually, Macready's box office scale was: Boxes and parquet, $1.00; amphitheatre, 50¢) and no mention of specific plays. This was in sharp contrast to Forrest's announcement, which was specific and informative—Broadway Theatre, name of play, and "Dress Circle and Parquette, 75¢; Family Circle and Upper Tiers, 25¢."

With Macready now on the battlegrounds and with Forrest playing to capacity at the Broadway, the theatrical news of the city centered on the two rivals, with the inevitable division of allegiances gaining in fervor each day. On the twenty-eighth the *Herald* offered a glowing tribute to Forrest's Damon (in *Damon and Pythias*), ". . . one of his best performances—one in which all that peculiar and brilliant genius and rich idiosyncrasy of talent which distinguish this great actor, is pre-eminently elicited. For ourselves as Americans, we prefer the unsophisticated energy of the daring child of nature to the more glossy polish of the artificial European civilian; yet each may be excellent in his own style, without collision. Some prefer the toga, some prefer the tomahawk." On Saturday, the twenty-eighth, Forrest performed *Jack Cade* and on Monday, *Lear,* both to good crowds and fine notices.

On Monday, April 30, the *Morning Express* gave a hint of the quality to be expected from Macready. "An excellent company is engaged to support him.—Chippendale, Sefton, and many more of the profession are in town, from the south, and several more are expected from day to day." No doubt this recruiting had been at the insistence of Macready. In this critical farewell engagement he must offer the best talent available.

May Day morning supplied an ominous chill for Macready, if a fire can be said to produce a chill. At 2:00 A.M. the guests of the New York Hotel were aroused by a blaze that had originated in the pantry and then spread to the dining room. Although there was an estimated damage of $15,000, no one was injured, and the guests were permitted to return to their beds. There was never any suggestion even from his most devoted followers that this was an attempt by Forrest's followers to burn Macready in his bed.

That same morning the *Morning Express* carried a long editorial which may have increased Macready's discomfiture by spreading further the already widespread knowledge of his difficulties with Forrest. The editorial, though it contained some inaccurate prognostications, provided one of the sanest appraisals of the situation ever to appear in print.

Mr. Forrest, now in the midst of a prosperous engagement at the Broadway Theatre, will, we have reason to believe, continue to act at that establishment during the greater portion, if not all, of Mr. Macready's engagement at the Opera House. Both will have large auditories, nightly; both will make money for themselves, and for their respective managements. This is as it should be.... There are those among us who imagine that there is likely to arise some ebullition of popular or partisan feeling on the opening night of Mr. Macready's new season in New York. We have no such fears. . . . Mr. Macready was imprudent and hasty in going out of his way to allude, on being called before the curtain, to fancied plots and conspiracies against him; and we think, he might as well have left the threat of a suit for libel unuttered. As to Mr. Forrest, we cannot but think now, as we have ever thought, that Mr. Macready has never been to him the 'rook ahead' which he would fain have his countrymen believe.

The article went on to appraise the various letters offered in evidence by the two men and then concluded with this paragraph: "There is something to forgive, and to be forgiven, on both sides, and each has an equal opportunity of evincing magnanimity and generosity, in being foremost to say 'forgive and forget.' The reconciliation of these two ornaments to a liberal profession would not only redound greatly to their own credit, but upon the profession, itself–It would gladden the hearts of 'troops of friends,' on both sides, and form another happy illustration of that rapid growth of good feeling, which is now eminently characterizing the intercourse between the mother and daughter land." Unfortunately, there was no evidence of "magnanimity and generosity" in the behavior of the principal parties or their adherents.

On Tuesday evening (May 1) Forrest performed *Jack Cade,* again to a large audience which, according to the *Herald* (May 2), was "delighted and greeted the expressions of liberal sentiment which he uttered from time to time, with great approbation." There can be no question of Forrest's triumphant command of his audiences during this engagement, but even so not all the notices carried unequivocal praise; e.g., "The horribly disfigured throat and face, and the final death gasp and gurgle are by no means pleasing though they may be very good counterfeits of the things which they represent." These comments, quoted from the *Herald* (May 3), were directed at his Spartacus in *The Gladiator,* which he had performed on May 2. And in his *Othello,* on the third, the *Herald* (May 4) found that "he so gesticulates and pauses, emphasizes and looks aghast, treads the stage heavily and stops suddenly, that he reaches his climax by a series of jerks." On Friday night, the fourth, he took a break, but the Saturday *Herald* kept his name in the theatrical news with a summary of his current engagement. "During the past week, Forrest has been playing in some of his finest parts, and the immense audience which have been gathered together on each evening, is proof enough of the high estimation he is held in by our most intellectual and prominent citizens. . . ." On Sunday morning, however, the *Herald* reviewer was back with a critical notice of Forrest's Saturday night performance of *Richard III.* "There was every now and then a burst of vehement passion, admirably given; yet these bursts seemed to be too uniform when they occurred, and to be saved and hoarded up, as it were, to bring out the telling parts, while all the rest of the character was played carelessly and negligently. We make these remarks in true regard for our great actor; we have lauded him beyond all other actors, but never meant thereby that he was beyond improvement." But no matter what questions were raised about his playing, Forrest was going strong as he began the fateful week of May 7 with another performance of *Macbeth*.

Macready meanwhile had been busy preparing for his opening and was apparently too occupied with his immediate concerns to indulge himself in any diatribes in his diary against the performances of his rival. But he could not ignore the newspaper reports concerning Forrest's relationship with his wife. "The tenderness of the American Press towards that scoundrel [Forrest] is an uncontradictable evidence of its rascality and baseness." On May 1 he reported to his diary that he had received what he took to be a subtle hint to leave the country. "An anonymous note in disguised hand, recommending me to send a challenge to Mr. Forrest to go and fight in Canada, assuring me he would not have the courage to go!!! Oh, clever gentleman!" On Wednesday the second, Macready gave some readings at the Hope Chapel at 720 Broadway for the "teachers of the common schools," with a special invitation "extended to the teachers of the public schools of Brooklyn." Macready may have wished to test the tenor of his New York audience under obviously favorable circumstances, or he may have wished to exhibit his superior talent for theatrical readings. On the previous Saturday he had dined with the David Coldens and had gone with them to hear Mrs. Butler (Fanny Kemble) read *King Henry VIII*. He had found the performance so abominable that he could not stay.

Macready favored the teachers with a potpourri of selections from *The Bible,* the fifth book of *Paradise Lost,* the fourth act of *Henry IV,* and a passage from a prose tale which none of the newspaper reporters could identify. According to the *Daily Tribune* (May 3), "these were read in Mr. Macready's usual excellent style, and the warmest mani-

MACREADY AS MACBETH

festations of applause greeted him at the close of each selection. . . . The attention of the audience was almost breathless." These kind words were small compensation for the columns of comment on his quarrel with Forrest.

During this week there was not a day that one of the newspapers did not carry a passage headed "Forrest and Macready," dealing with one or another aspect of the controversy. On May 2 the *Herald* returned to the subject of Henry Wikoff. "The whole dispute has been fomented by a malicious little Iago, who has been offended with Macready and has attempted to work up and excite Forrest, in order to gratify his own petty, venomous, little malice." The *Herald* suggested "that the mutual friends of these two great men should, in some way or other, have a meeting and confer together upon this controversy, hear both sides, receive mutual explanations, and, should a reconciliation of these unhappy disputes between them be the result, it would certainly be better for both of them, than to remain in the position in which we have seen them for some time past—writing the hardest and bitterest things against each other. Let us see if we cannot produce some sort of pacification, by some such negotiation." At first glance one might have expected Macready to accept this as a judgment in his behalf. He did not take it so. In his diary entry for that evening he wrote, "An article headed with that disgusting beginning, *Forrest and Macready*. It is really too bad. In it this Bennett turns his dislike to Forrest and his vulgar aversion to me into a concentrated spite against Wikoff, charging on him all this Forrest's villainy, and strongly recommending the intermediation of friends to make up this 'difference' (!!!) between us! Is it thus these wretches contemplate such open violation of truth, honesty, and every bond that claims respect!"

Neither Macready nor Forrest was in any mood for appeasement as they both sat out Sunday waiting to begin their respective *Macbeths* on Monday night (May 7).

If the two managements had any fears of trouble, these were lost in the happy assurance of a full house at each establishment. As the *Herald* had glowingly reported on May 3, "Everything is flourishing in New York. Trade is brisk, industry is productive, the shipping interests are going ahead, and theatricals flourish along side all these elements of general prosperity."

Though operating on a lower admission scale than that proposed by Macready, Forrest had been prospering at the Broadway. In two weeks the box-office receipts had reached nearly $9,000. Half of this had gone into Forrest's pocket, and the other half was divided among the manager, the other actors, the scene-shifters, and miscellaneous functionaries.

Nor was theatrical prosperity limited to the Broadway. Thomas Hamblin, after the Park Theatre had burned down, on December 16, 1848, had taken over the management of the Bowery and was well on his way to accumulating his "third or fourth fortune made in the exercise of his profession." Even before Hamblin came to the Bowery, it had had a reputation as a "cool, steady, and permanent" moneymaker. Burton's Chambers Street Theatre had also had a successful season, relying almost entirely on John Brougham's dramatization of Dicken's *Dombey and Son*. The National was making its fortune with the amusing escapades of Chanfrau's "Mose"; and Barnum's American Museum, the Olympic Theatre, and Christy's Minstrels, at Mechanics' Hall, had drawn their share of theatrical business for the 1848–49 season.

Eggs à la Montreal

CHAPTER SEVEN

The Astor Place Opera House had been leased for Macready's engagement by Colonel William Niblo and James H. Hackett. Niblo was the proprietor of Niblo's Gardens, an establishment which had been famous since 1830 for its summer season of light comedies and variety entertainments. Hackett was best known for his impersonation of Falstaff in *The Merry Wives of Windsor.* The previous summer the two men had leased the Opera House for a warm-weather season of Viennese dancers, singers, and farces. John Sefton and William Chippendale, who

ASTOR PLACE OPERA HOUSE

had been hired as stage director and manager, respectively, for Macready's new engagement, had also been associated with the previous summer's venture.

Niblo was really marking time with his new enterprise. He was supervising the construction of a new theatre and hotel on the grounds of his Gardens at Broadway and Prince Street, an elegant establishment that was to be ready for a spectacular opening with the Ravel Troupe on July 30, 1849. Hackett had made a quick shift from actor to proprietor. In fact, he had just completed a six nights' engagement at the Broadway the day before Forrest moved into that theatre.

In leasing the Astor Place Opera House, Niblo and Hackett were obviously ignoring the bad luck that had besieged the house from its opening. The building had been completed in 1847, its construction having been financed by subscriptions obtained from a group of "wealthy aspirers to fashion," and was named after John Jacob Astor, who had developed the neighborhood and who, until his death in 1848, maintained his residence nearby at 37 Lafayette Place. The relatively new opera house, or theatre, had had its grand opening on November 22, 1847, with a production of Verdi's *Ernani* under the management of Sanquirico and Patti. It was actually used both as a theatre and an opera house, but the managers, apparently feeling that the latter term was more elegant and perhaps deferring to a lingering prejudice against theatres, preferred "opera house." In any case, everything had been tastefully arranged with a view to making the 1,800 patrons feel that they were in *the* high-toned theatrical and operatic establishment of the city. As the opening playbill specified, "No lady [was] admitted unaccompanied by a gentleman." The admission scale was $1.00 for the boxes, parquet, and balcony, and 50¢ for the amphitheatre (a narrow, steep gallery just under the ceiling). New York society was out in force on the first night, and, according to one reporter, "a generally diffused air of good breeding pervaded the entire atmosphere." But with all this elegance, the first season ended "with dissension among the singers and with insolvency on the part of the management." The individual dramatic engagements that followed did somewhat better, but the next season of opera was as poor as the first, ending, according to the New York *Herald* (May 3) with "a dead loss of $20,000 and $900 due to some of the chorus singers." This was the record of the enterprise when Niblo and Hackett took over as lessees.

They felt confident, however, that the general prosperity of the New York theatre, plus the special attraction that Macready was expected to exert, would override any ill luck that might still be pursuing the Astor Place Opera House. New York theatres were, indeed, during this spring season of 1849, demonstrating a phenomenal vitality. For Monday night, the seventh of May, three *Macbeth*s were announced: Macready at the Astor Place Opera House, Forrest at the Broadway, and Hamblin at the Bowery. The National offered *The Enchanter, or The Wizard of the Mountain,* and Burton's, an operatic burlesque entitled *Herr Nanny*. Also available were Signor Francisco's nightly seance at Bleecker Hall and, in the Assembly Rooms of the Chinese Museum, Voightlander's Microcosmic Views of Scenes in Italy, Germany, Spain, *et al*. Apparently there were more than enough spectators to go around, although the two principal *Macbeth*s were unquestionably the centers of theatrical attention.

There was excitement—and a degree of anticipation—in the air on Monday. No one seems to have had any organized plan, apart from ordering out a few policemen to be on hand at the Opera House, but the press reflected a rising ferment.

During the last thirty-six hours the excitement among the theatre-going people has been rising to fever heat in this atmosphere. Forrest plays at the Broadway, Macready at the Astor Place, and Hamblin at the Bowery. The excitement began in the green room, and has been generating for some time, in consequence of the public attitude of the two great tragedians of the age towards each others, and their appearance in this city at the same time, in the same characters, at different theatres. Hamblin, with his usual tact, was determined not to allow Forrest and Macready to have all the fun and dollars to themselves, so he put in his oar, and has come out with the same tragedy in a new cast, thus increasing the general sensation which this singular conjunction of events is calculated to produce among theatrical people.

This singular theatrical excitement and enterprise springs up, too, at a very curious time in this metropolis, namely, at the time of the anniversaries of all the religious, philosophical, moral, sentimental and socialist societies. It will be a great week in New York. [What a prophecy!] The streets will be crowded with parsons and play-actors, and play-goers and philosophers, beyond anything ever seen before.

Throughout the rest of the article, the *Herald* (May 7) was inclined to depreciate the threat of violence.

So much is the sensation gradually increasing in reference to this matter, that the quarrel between Forrest and Macready, upon which so much has been said to little purpose, is almost forgotten, and begins to be considered an antiquated affair. It is impossible to get up a row at all about it. Among the frequenters of the theatres, and particularly the critical portion of them, there is great difference of opinion as to what actor will have the greatest attraction, and bring together the largest houses, and bag the greatest amount of dollars. At all events, it will be a curious night at the three great theatres this evening.

Most of the papers, not wishing to be accused of fomenting a disturbance, tried to minimize the dangers. The *Evening Post* (May 7), stated: "All thoughts of any personal difficulties between these two great tragedians will be merged in the anticipated pleasure of listening to and witnessing the high character of artistic skill exhibited in the interpretation of this historical drama." The correspondent for the Philadelphia *Ledger* wrote rather ambiguously of the coming performance and concluded with a comment on the weather. "The great theatrical warfare, which begins tonight is the leading topic of town conversation to-day. This triangular [Hamblin included] is expected to be productive of curious incidents during the evening—and not of the most felicitous character, either. The weather, however, is exceedingly unpleasant, threatening all three houses with a beggarly account of empty boxes."

The newspapers carried advertisements for both of the major attractions. Forrest's advertisement merely announced the event—doors open at seven o'clock, performance "to commence at 7½," prices, 75¢ and 25¢. Macready's listed the entire cast: Mr. Wemyss as Duncan, C. W. Clarke as Macduff, Mrs. Coleman Pope as Lady Macbeth, and W. Chippendale and John Sefton as Witches; prices, $1.00 and 50¢, doors open at seven, curtain to rise at eight o'clock.

During the day Macready "rehearsed with much care, looked at the papers, rested" and then went early to the theatre. He noted in his diary that when he arrived, "My hairdresser told me there would be a good house, for there was—an unusual sight—a great crowd outside." Inside the theatre Chief of Police Matsell was busy stationing his deputies.

One account, perhaps of doubtful authenticity, described the scene before the rise of the curtain.

At an early hour the theatre was crowded, and the gallery presented a sinister and ominous appearance. Long before the rise of the curtain the regular "tramp, tramp, tramp," so peculiar to the frequenters of the Chatham and Bowery theatres, could be heard in the gallery, which was densely packed. It was a warning note to the managers, who were in consultation on the stage. Hackett pulled aside the green curtain and took a hasty survey of the scene. Turning to Officer Bowyer of the chief's staff, who was immediately behind him he said:

"This looks rather dubious, Mr. Bowyer!"

"Yes," was the reply; "The b'hoys are here assuredly! What induced you to sell so many tickets? [Many more tickets were sold than there were seats.] People are making a tremendous rush at the doors yet, and the house is full—over full—already."

The time for the performance approached, and at this moment the orchestra was rung in and commenced the overture, but still the steady "tramp, tramp, tramp" was heard, not alone in the gallery, but in other parts of the house.

"What do you think, Mr. Bowyer," queries Hackett. "Do you imagine there is going to be a disturbance?"

"There is mischief in the parquet and gallery," responds the officer, "but probably no actual violence will be attempted. The b'hoys will make a noise and endeavor to prevent the play proceeding, but possibly will do nothing further. They seem to be patient and very good natured; but Mr. Macready may expect a rough reception."

There is a momentary lull in the demonstrations in the parquet and gallery, and the curtain is "rung up" on the three witches, and their scene. Mr. Clarke as Macduff, a popular favorite and American, was received with vociferous applause.

Macready, who was below stage, misunderstood this applause. According to his diary, he smiled and said to himself, "They mistake him for me." How wrong he was. Macready used the common nineteenth-century acting version of

Macbeth in which Ross's lines in Act I, scene 2, are given to Macduff. In Shakespeare's text, of course, Macduff does not appear until Act II, scene 3. When the third scene of Act I began, and Macready's voice was heard offstage with, "Command they make a halt upon the heath!" the crowd was ready for him. Handkerchiefs were waved by some ladies in the boxes, but there was also, commingled with cheers, a loud storm of groans and hisses—"an alarming outbreak that defies description." At first Macready's supporters seemed to be in the majority, but the anti-Macreadyites made up in noise for what they lacked in numbers. Bill Wilson, a prize fighter who was also, apparently, one of the leaders, threw out a banner in front of the gallery, bearing on one side the words, "No apologies, it is too late," and on the other, "You have proved yourself a liar!" As Macready stood in defiant silence, the b'hoys began to pelt him with "eggs of doubtful purity, potatoes, a bottle of pungent and nauseating asafoetida, old shoes, and a copper coin." Macready stooped and picked up the coin and "placed it in his bosom with dignity" and then with "mock humiliation bowed to the quarter of the gallery from which the visitation had descended." For fifteen minutes there was no action on the stage. One gentleman in the parquet examined the house through a stupendous eyeglass large enough for a horse collar, and others "threw themselves into a variety of attitudes, more picturesque than becoming."

Macready walked forward to address the audience, intending to say, according to his account, "I felt pain and shame, which the intelligent and respectable must feel for their country's reputation, and that I would instantly resign my engagement rather than encounter such disgraceful conduct." But the attempt was futile; he returned to his position and advised his fellow players to "go on." The play was continued in "dumb show" while the shouts kept up. Rotten eggs *"a la Montreal,"* potatoes, and asafoetida were "dispensed profusely over the actors creating a most repulsive stench throughout the house." Macready "looked directly at these men as they committed these outrages, no way moved by them." The pantomimic performance of the first act was finally concluded and the curtain brought down.

An account of the intermission following the first act was given in the *Morning Express* (May 9):

... several gentlemen in the boxes undertook to remonstrate with that party of rioters who were in the parquette. Among them we noticed John Neal, the poet-barrister of Portland, Me. who happened to be in one of the first seats, near the stage. Rising and taking off his hat, he proceeded to address the "gentlemen" in the parquette, in good set terms, (we suppose: for it was all as much "dumb show" to us, as was Macready's *Macbeth*) and with much impassioned gesticulation. He had not proceeded long before he was interrupted by someone exclaiming, amidst roars of laughter, "When you're done your sermon, we'll go to prayer, old boy!" Another shouted, "Let's have a song first!" and at this the whole lot went at it at the top of their lungs. They sang a methodistical hymn, with a roaring chorus, meanwhile stamping and dancing —(many of them) upon the red plush chairs of the parquette.

Meanwhile, the editor of an evening paper meeting a distinguished leader of the Empire Club, in the lobby, playfully remarked, "So this is your doing, is it?" Upon which the "Captain" hit him a back-handed blow in the face.

A Mr. Strahan, (a Tammany Hall ground-tier orator), rose, towards the last, in the upper part of the parquette, and shouted, "Boys! three cheers for Edwin Forrest," which were given with a will. He then rose again, and with peculiar meaning said, "And now, boys, hurrah for *the seats!*" This implied proposition was received in silence.

Behind the scenes, some of the actors, according to Mac-

ready, "attempted to exhibit sympathy, which I received very
loftily, observing, 'My concern was for the disgrace such
people inflicted on the character of the country.'" Many of
the actors were loath to continue ducking the debris, but
Macready insisted that the performance should continue.

The second act went as the first, shouts accompanied with
vegetables. The crowd called to the other actors to quit the
stage. When, in the third act, Macbeth came on as the new
King, the uproar reached a new pitch, as if in response to a
supremely intolerable insult. Potatoes and asafoetida were
judged too mild. A group of men in the easterly corner of
the upper tier threw four chairs in rapid succession. The
first of these landed in the orchestra and "caused a prestis-
simo movement among the musicians, not set down in the
original music for *Macbeth*." The second landed at the feet
of Mrs. Pope, and the other two narrowly missed Macready
and splintered about the stage. Macready bowed to the audience and then "going up to Mr. Chippendale, observed
that I thought 'I had quite fulfilled my obligation to Messrs.
Niblo and Hackett, and that I should now remain no
longer.'" The curtain was rung down, and the rioters were
left in command.

Mr. Chippendale came forward to address the crowd, but,
unable to get a single word out above the bedlam, he retired
behind the scenes. Fifteen minutes later, the noise still continuing, Chippendale and Sefton came forward with a piece
of canvas on which was written in chalk, "Mr. Macready has
left the theatre." The mob answered with a banner of their
own inscribed, "No apologies! It is too late!" Mr. Clarke, the
Macduff of the evening, then came before the curtain at the
request of Mr. Chippendale. The crowd quieted for a moment while Clarke, an American, assured them that Macready had indeed left the theatre. Someone in the audience

then asked Clarke why he was there. Clarke replied that he was there "in the discharge of the duties of his profession, by which he lived and supported his family." Although Clarke was greeted with applause, there were some who felt that he was presenting himself as an "apologist" for Macready. Clarke was forced to resort to the press a few days later to clear up his position.

The audience, although generally not blaming Clarke, felt that they had been outsmarted by Macready. John Ryder (previously mentioned in connection with the Edinburgh hiss) had been Macready's regular Macduff, having played the part in the previous American performances; but Macready had felt that he might temper the anti-British feeling, at least to some degree, by introducing an American Macduff. Accordingly, Ryder had gone down to the Bowery to give one performance as Macduff in Hamblin's *Macbeth*.

After Clarke's speech the evening was concluded with a half-hour repetition of the familiar battle cries: "Three groans for the English bulldog!" "Nine cheers for Edwin Forrest!" "Down with the codfish aristocracy!" "Take off the Devonshire bull!" "Huzza for native talent!"

Although there was obviously an organized force in attendance at the theatre—the notorious Captain Rynders later admitted that he had purchased fifty tickets and distributed them among his friends; and Chief of Police Matsell reported that some five hundred people were engaged in the disturbance—there was no attempt by the police to quell the riot or to make any arrests. Someone said later that the rioters had even prepared papers of gunpowder to throw into the magnificent chandelier. With their bold defiance of the authorities, they had certainly won the day. According to one reporter, "At the end of the evening one of the rowdies marched down from the theatre and treated his disor-

derly gang to champagne at a hotel, manifestly at the expense of persons concealed."

But if one accepts Macready's account, he seems not to
have been totally dismayed.

Colden seemed to apprehend danger out of doors; I did not.
However, I took my dirk, but thinking it unworthy to carry it,
threw it down again. Colden (who made too much of it), Tallmadge and Emmett walked home with me; there was no sign of
any attempt in the back street, but there was a crowd at the front
door, which Colden had not been able to penetrate, and which,
the Chief of the Police informed me afterwards, made the strongest efforts to break into the house. I was in the best spirits, and we
talked over what was to be done. A Mr. Bennett—stranger—
came, as he said, from young Astor and other names of the first,
he said, to say that this should be resisted, and to convey to me
the expression of their regret. Mr. Monnitt, my landlord, and one
of the heads of the police called, to show me a deposition taken
from one of the rioters who had been captured, and who, because
he cried very much, was set at liberty. I asked leave to copy the
deposition and I am about to do it, and I suppose shall have a
long night's writing. And this is my treatment! Being left alone, I
begin to feel more seriously the indignities put on me, and en-
tertain ideas of not going on the stage. Pray God I may do what is
right. I will try to do so. I thank His goodness that I am safe and
unharmed. Wrote to dearest Catherine.

The *Macbeth*s at the other theatres had fared much better.
At the Bowery the audience "was crammed in every part;
and what is more, the entire audience was composed of a
most brilliant assemblage of our most intelligent citizens."
This and the following reports are from the *Herald* of the
next day. "As often as we have seen Mr. Hamblin perform
the part, we have never seen him do it better than last evening. . . . Mrs. Shaw as Lady Macbeth was truly great." Even
Macready's British actor, Ryder, was marked as an "admi-

rable performer." At the conclusion of the tragedy Hamblin appeared before the curtain to address the crowd with these words: "Who says the love of the drama and Shakespeare's plays is dead in New York? This (pointing to the vast audience) is my reply. If you, ladies and gentlemen, will continue to act your part as well as you have done this evening, and thus support it, I promise to produce the plays in a style never before seen in this city."

At the Broadway, about a mile downtown from Astor Place, Forrest was "greeted with a magnificent house, consisting of a large portion of elegantly dressed ladies, and never did he play better. This great American tragedian delineated the character of Macbeth in a style of unsurpassed beauty, and the bursts of applause which followed from the enraptured audience was truly astonishing, as well as it must have been gratifying to Mr. Forrest." When he came to the lines "What rhubarb, senna, or what purgative drug/Would scour these English hence?" the whole audience rose and cheered frantically.

The National had its largest crowd of the season for a performance of *The Enchanter,* an elaborate spectacle which one reporter commented on with unqualified approval: "Never in all our theatre-going (which is not trifling) did we ever see such beautiful scenery as was displayed last night —such pleasant processions, such elegant tableaux." The operatic "burletta" at Burton's, *Herr Nanny,* had a "patient and numerous audience but was not much appreciated." Voightlander's Microcosmic Views at the Chinese Museum came off with "great éclat, and to the evident satisfaction of a brilliant and fashionable assembly. These magical pictures are reflected through two gigantic thirteen inch lenses by the aid of Professor Grant's improved hydro-oxygen light, upon a transparent screen, thirty feet square. We do not know any way in which an hour or two can be more agreeably spent, than in witnessing this eminently beautiful and novel exhibition."

A large share of the New York population must have been away from home that Monday evening. Those not at the theatre were in attendance at one of the Anniversary Week meetings around the city. The Society for the Abolition of Capital Punishment, The Methodist Episcopal Church Missionary Society, The American Seamen's Friend Society, and The American Protestant Society all had sessions that evening. These assemblies, continuing their meetings straight through the week, were also troubled by the rowdies. On Tuesday morning Captain Rynders and his crew, still glowing with their success at the Opera House the night before, broke up the meeting of the American Anti-Slavery Society at the Broadway Tabernacle; and in the afternoon of the same day they made an unsuccessful attempt to disrupt the proceedings of the American and Foreign Anti-Slavery Society in the same building. This was a week for "causes" of all kinds and for the free and easy expression of opinion.

On Tuesday, May 8, the newspapers were filled with accounts of the Opera House disturbance, but most of them, waiting to see how things were going to shake down, delayed their editorial comments until the following day. The *Courier and Enquirer,* however, spoke out immediately in condemnation of Forrest. "With his peculiar tastes he will probably enjoy the infamy, and deem it a triumph. The cost of the victory—now that he has reduced his household expenses—he probably will not feel. That his proceedings will diminish the number of his own admirers, it would probably be perilous to predict; but their effect upon the *character* of his circle of friends, will not be doubtful." This short item was to cause quite a stir the next day.

While most of the editorialists were temporarily side-stepping the issue, the merchants were meeting it squarely in the advertising columns of the city's newspapers. Under the heading "MUSICAL./FORREST AND MAC-READY," one advertisement declared, "They are certainly eminent as Tragedians" and continued, "Jacots of 35 Chatham street, and 190 Canal street, is equally eminent as the vendor of Accordions, Violins, Flutes, and Musical Instruments; also Watches, Jewelry, and fancy goods." There followed a "certified" record of orders and sales:

"Monday, April 23—Sold 5,000,000 Accordions, 95,000 Violins, 300,000 gold breast pins and 1 Jews' Harp.

"Tuesday—Sold, one gold Watch, one Flute, one Guitar, one Tamourine [sic], and 399,999 Violin Strings.

"Wednesday—Received an order from California for any quantity of Magnifying Glasses, for the purpose of finding gold in larger quantities.

"Implicit reliance can be placed on the above statements. Those who are sceptical will please call and be convinced."

Macready, however, was not taking the proceedings so lightly. When he arose on Tuesday morning, he was determined to get out of the country as soon as possible. He informed Hackett that he considered himself absolved from any engagement and that he should not appear again at the Opera House. Indeed, he would not even remain for his scheduled sailing on June 7; he sent to the steamship *America* to book immediate passage to England. During the day a number of persons of "highest respectability, in and out of official station" called upon him with assurances that public opinion was entirely on the side of law and order in condemnation of his assailants. If he would agree to appear again, he could be certain that there would be no further disturbance, at least none that could not be checked by the

police. Macready, not without reason, continued to hesitate.
Not until evening, when he received the following letter,
signed by forty-seven prominent citizens, did he finally
capitulate.

> DEAR SIR: The undersigned, having heard that the outrage at
> the Astor Place Opera House, on Monday evening, is likely to
> have the effect of preventing you from concluding your in-
> tended farewell engagement on the American stage, take this
> public method of requesting you to reconsider your decision,
> and of assuring you that the good sense and respect for order
> prevailing in this community will sustain you on the subse-
> quent nights of your performance.

Included among the signers were Washington Irving,
Evert A. Duyckinck, and Herman Melville. Macready
agreed to appear again, but he believed that his second performance should be postponed until Friday. He evidently
expected the excitement to subside by then, and he wanted
time for the circulation of certain documents in his behalf.
His friends insisted, however, that the present state of public
opinion was so entirely on the side of order "that a delay so
long as Friday might cause a relaxation, and give opportunity to turbulent spirits to attempt breaches of the peace."
Macready compromised on Thursday.

The documents which he wished to circulate were, of
course, his own. Since the previous November he had been
collecting letters. In fact, he already had them in print and
was awaiting only the appropriate moment to release them.
Even before seeking passage that morning, he had prepared
a foreword for these documents and had arranged to have
them distributed by the printers, Stringer and Townsend,
under the title *The Replies From England, etc., To certain
statements circulated in This Country respecting Mr. MAC-
READY*. Included were copies of Forrest's statements to the

press and letters from Bulwer-Lytton, Forster, Fonblanque,
John Mitchell (lessee of the St. James Theatre), Charles Bass
(the comedian), and Macready's counsel, William B. Reed,
of Philadelphia.

In the foreword Macready explained that he had deferred
to the opinion of his legal advisers "to reply in silence upon
the generally expressed disbelief of the said charges; at the
same time purposing to leave with his friends the means of
vindicating his character, and their own confidence in it
(should it hereafter be called in question), he arranged the
answers returned to him from England with the intention
of printing a certain number of copies for private distribu-
tion. The outrages of Monday evening make it necessary to
give publicity to them, which he does in the exact form in
which they were prepared for circulation among his
friends." These remarks, which were dated May 8, 1849,
were, of course, unfortunately timed. If Forrest's friends had
any inclination to rest their case with their success of Monday night in driving Macready from the stage, their antagonism was revived by the appearance of Macready's *Replies*.

On the same day a new common council and a new mayor
were sworn in at twelve noon, retiring Mayor Havemeyer
administering the oath of office. "You, Caleb S. Woodhull,
do solemnly swear that you will faithfully support the Con-
stitution of the United States and of the State of New York,
and that you will administer the duties of the office of Mayor
of the City of New York to the best of your abilities. So help
you, God." Woodhull said that he did; he was soon to regret
this statement.

On Tuesday night the Astor Place Opera House was dark,
but the Bowery offered *Othello* with Hamblin as the Moor
and Ryder as Iago. Forrest was on in *Richelieu* at the Broad-

way with a performance that "stood out in strong and bold relief in all the phases of the subtle character." The original schedule at the Opera House had called for Macready to perform the same play on Tuesday evening. At the same time *The Enchanter* was playing at the National, *Romance and Reality,* at Burton's, and, elsewhere in the city, three minstrel troupes—Christy's, Campbell's, and the New Orleans Serenaders.

On Wednesday the papers were filled with comments on the events of Monday night and their aftermath. Both the *Morning Express* and the *Evening Post* dwelt on the slanderous attack on Forrest which had appeared in the *Courier and Enquirer* the day before. According to the *Post,*

A scandalous charge was preferred against Mr. Forrest yesterday in a morning paper. No man who is in the least acquainted with the character of Mr. Forrest, and he has been long enough before the public to have given them some knowledge of his personal qualities, could possibly have brought himself to believe him guilty of a course, to say nothing of it in other respects, so unmanly and cowardly towards a professional rival. The libel in question occasioned the following letter from Mr. Forrest's legal adviser:

No. 56 WALL STREET, May 8, 1849

To THE PROPRIETOR OF THE COURIER AND ENQUIRER:

I am desired by Mr. Forrest, to call your attention to the article in your paper of this day's date, in which you have seen fit to charge him with participation in the disturbances that took place last evening, at the Astor Place Opera House.

I am instructed to say that every charge against Mr. Forrest contained in the article in question is absolutely and grossly false, and as the attack is coupled with reflections of a most improper and offensive character, I hope that you will see the propriety of retracting and withdrawing the accusation in the most immediate, direct, and ample manner.

The charges which you have made, are of the most serious description, and you will, I am satisfied, see the propriety and justice of this demand.

I am respectfully,
Your obd't serv't,
THEODORE SEDGWICK."

The *Courier and Enquirer* backed down in their issue of May 9, adding that the offending "paragraph was published without the knowledge of the responsible editor, who does not deem the facts sufficient to warrant the assertion. The other papers carried their own views of the breakdown of law and order. The New York *Tribune* dwelt on the rights of the spectator and the professional actor and on the need for a reasonable understanding of freedom and democracy; the *Morning Express* expounded on the inefficiency of the police; and the *Herald* was disposed to take things rather lightheartedly.

Some excerpts will suggest what the talk of the town must have been from Tuesday to Thursday. An article in the *Tribune* (May 9) was headed, "The Outrage on Macready," and began, without partisanship, "Mr. Macready is an English play-actor; Mr. Edwin Forrest an American ditto; and each is eminent in their miserable vocation." Concerning the violence on Monday night:

A more wanton, tyrannous and scoundrelly outrage than this we could not well conceive. It was in the first place a cowardly theft of the money which the quiet portion of the audience had paid for the expected pleasure of seeing the play. . . . Whoever is let into another's house for a certain specific purpose is really there under a compact to do nothing inconsistent with the rights of others therein, or with the accomplishment of the purpose for which it is opened to visitors. To suppose that, because a man has paid a dollar at the door, he is therefore entitled to annoy and

alarm his fellow-visitors, to put a stop to the performance, destroy
the furniture and endanger the limbs of the performers, is to
evince an intensity of stupidity and ruffianism which even "Mose"
[a popular stage comic] should be ashamed of.

Mr. Macready is a player by profession; to drive him from the
stage is in principle to doom him to starve. True, he may have
money laid up, of which we know nothing; but that does not affect the principle above enunciated. To drive him from the stage
is to say,

> Though he wishes to play and must do so to live,
> · and though there are thousands who wish to see
> · and hear him play on the terms proffered, yet
> · we of our sovereign pleasure will not permit that
> · reciprocity of benefits to be effected. Though
> · we be but forty, and those who wish to listen and
> · enjoy be a thousand, yet we will break up the
> · performance by yelling and rioting, driving off
> · the players by showers of offensive and dangerous missiles!

And yet every one of the miscreants who practice this atrocious
and impudent tyranny will boast of his readiness to fight for
Liberty, and is ready to knock any smaller man down who in-
sinuates aught against his Democracy. They can't imagine any
better Democrat than they are, unless it be Forrest.

When will the stage, that vaunted school of Morality, that ful-
some adulator and systematic corrupter of Popular Liberty, begin
to teach its votaries clearer and truer ideas of Freedom? If the
Theater is not to be given up as essentially and incurably vicious
and vitiating, is it not high time for it to teach nobler lessons and
juster principles than those exemplified in the outrage on Macready?

The *Morning Express* (May 9) quoted the letter to Macready from Irving and the others and then expanded on
the agents of law-enforcement.

There was no fact more prominent, upon that occasion, than the utter inefficiency of the Police, which was present in considerable force, but without doing anything whatever towards preventing or stopping the riot. We heard this answer given by one of the principal policemen, when asked why there was no interference on their part, to put a stop to the proceedings at their height.

"Oh! It's a *general* thing!" as if it were the doing of the whole audience, and as if they had a perfect right to do it! The pretext that there were no overt acts of criminality, of breach of the peace, was thus thinly covered over, either by the pusillanimity or, what we fear is more likely, the sympathy of those whose duty it was to take notice of them and to arrest their perpetrators. . . .

Although unwilling to accept the view that "a citizen in the position of Mr. Forrest could deliberately plan, or even give his assent to, transactions like those of Monday night," the *Express* insisted that Macready deserved to be protected, no matter who instigated the attacks upon him, by "due execution of the laws of the country in which he is sojourn-ing. And the lessees of the theatre, at which he is engaged— who pay to the city a regular license, and are doubly entitled to its protection, have their rights too, in which they can equitably claim to be maintained by its ordinances."

The *Herald* (May 9) preferred to poke fun at the affair:

Undoubtedly, these occurrences ought to be deprecated. They were much more heavy than agreeable—much more disreputable than dignified. But human nature is a singular commodity, and is pretty much the same in all great cities. Philosophy must not go off in hysterics at every little outburst of human emotion—par-ticularly of theatrical human emotion. New York, in the present jocund month of May, is not alone distinguished for theatrical explosions of feeling. London has, in times not yet wholly for-gotten, earned a very respectable reputation in the same way; and we ourselves have had, before Monday last, a few extraordinary lively melo-dramas, "got up expressly for the occasion." Indeed, we think that the theatrical riots in London—the famous O. P. riots, for instance—were more formidable than anything we have ever been able to get up here, even with the best "native talent." We generally content ourselves with pantomime and farce. Our amiable brethren, on the other side of the water, like to sprinkle their performances in this way with a dash of tragedy, broken skulls and bloody noses. In fact, since the days when the "b'hoys" of Athens attempted to settle the business of Mr. McAristophanes for his attack on their favorite Cleon, theatrical audiences in all countries have assumed the right of expressing their sovereign wrath and displeasure. In this respect, John Bull and Brother Jonathan have both, at times, been very naughty and generally look silly when they wake up next morning.

The *Herald* could not, however, accept the notion that Forrest was the instigator of the revolt. "We regard such accusations as gratuitous and unjustifiable. Where is the evidence that Mr. Forrest had any personal agency in the disturbance? Perhaps he does not regret it very much; and his cards and letters may have waked up the 'b'hoys' to work, but that is all."

The rest of the article was devoted to background details. "Here, we think, it may not be amiss to give the public a little insight into the origin of all these difficulties. The public have been, heretofore, a good deal in the dark on this subject. A brief statement of the facts will be at once instructive and edifying. It is a discreditable business all round— and the saddle should be put on the right horse."

Forrest's first visit to England was accompanied (according to the *Herald*) by "generous feelings" both on the part of Macready and Forrest; the troubles had really started with Dickens.

This next chapter in the astounding History, which beats "Plutarch's Lives" all to pieces, opens with the visit of "Boz," alias

Dickens, to the United States. Some aged inhabitants probably yet recollect the excruciating fuss which was made about the talented little Cockney in this metropolis. The ball at the Park Theatre capped the climax, and the popular enthusiasm then reached its culminating point. Poor Dickens was bamboozled, bewildered, stunned, deafened, and quite overwhelmed by this foretaste of the apotheosis of the "universal nation," and he almost nodded his well perfumed head off his shoulders, in reply to the salutations of the New York aristocracy, of all shades, castes, shapes, and dimensions; from codfish up to salt pork, "Boz" was, like the prophet's ass elevated to the seventeenth heaven. Next day, he awoke. He found out that it was all a capital hoax—a farce—a flam. The ball had been gotten up to put a few thousand dollars into the dilapidated treasury of the Park Theatre! Horror and agony! Here was the funny, quizzical, extravagant, rollicking, whimsical, riotous "jollification," which New York knew how to get up for its own amusement, the benefit of the Park Theatre, and the utter and desolating bewilderment of the illustrious, miraculous, and never-to-be-forgotten "Boz."

"Boz" raved, and wrote his book. The iron had entered into his soul. On his return to London, he was affectionately embraced by his literary associates, Forster, Fonblanque, Lemon, and others of that ilk and with them over innumerable pots of the "heavy wet," he whined forth the agony of his wounded spirit. Grief is contagious and the little coterie whined in sympathy. . . . Just at this moment, while Forster, "Boz," and their associates of the London press were red-hot against everything American, Mr. Forrest made his second visit to the English metropolis. Then appeared the unfriendly notices, and then were made the attempts to hiss him off the stage. The whole opposition to him originated with this little knot of *literatteurs,* inflamed against the United States, on account of the sad treatment of their "pal" and brother, Master "Boz." We have never believed that Mr. Macready originated or stimulated the attacks on Forrest at that time. He is perfectly innocent on that score, notwithstanding Forrest's belief and interminable letters in bad taste to the contrary.

"Now comes another chapter, and the last. When Mr. Macready came to this country, Wikoff—the Chevalier Wikoff—*the* Wikoff —who had in vain attempted to fawn on Macready in London, one of the Dickens' clique—and obtain a gracious smile, or even a patronizing kick from that awful personage, instilled into Mr. Forrest's ear the poisonous insinuations which we have exposed not long since. Wikoff's story, every word of which was pure invention, was the principal foundation on which Forrest has felt and acted. Then came the "cards" and speeches, and thus the quarrel proceeded.

Well, both sides seem to be about even. The books are balanced, and we hope that they will be at once closed, and a new account opened. "Boz" on one side, and the New York "b'hoys" on the other, have "said their say." Dickens wrote his book; full of genius, and description, and humor, and pathos, and sentiment, and silliness; the "b'hoys" have produced their travesty of *Macbeth,* and the efforts of both cliques should now cease. A great decisive battle has been fought. The sun has set on the field of Waterloo. Let a treaty of peace be made, signed, and ratified, with all the solemnity befitting the occasion. Bring forth the calumet of peace, and let us, "To-morrow to fresh fields and pastures new." . . . Let the New York "b'hoys" show the civilized world, that if they can rival any London audience in riot, disorder and disgrace to-day— they can also far surpass them in generosity and justice on the third day thereafter. We must not allow Macready to return to England without settling old scores, and opening a new set of books.

These views were not, unfortunately, shared by Forrest's adherents. The escapade of Monday night had merely whetted their appetites.

Macready, however, knew only what he heard from his friends and what he read in the press. On Wednesday morning he replied to Irving and his fellow-signers:

DEAR SIRS,—I have the honor of acknowledging your obliging letter. It is one I find some difficulty in answering.

Under the unprovoked indignities offered me in the Astor Place Theatre, it was certainly my desire and my fixed purpose to avail myself of the legal right thus afforded me, and withdraw at once from my engagement contracted there.

In leaving this country, which has been endeared to my recollection by long and strong attachments, I should not have done you the injustice of associating the American character with the ill-deed of persons, unhappily too frequently to be found in every large community: and in that same spirit which would preserve me from a hasty and inconsiderate judgment upon the late occurrence, I assent to your request, honoring and feeling grateful for the sentiment that has dictated it.

I remain, dear sirs, most faithfully yours,

W. C. MACREADY

NEW YORK HOTEL, MAY 9, 1849.

The English actor was certain that the "best citizens" and all the forces of law and order were exercising themselves in his behalf and that to play out his engagement would establish once and for all his superiority to the American scoundrel and his ill-bred supporters.

All the New York managers seem to have profited by the full columns of "theatrical intelligence" devoted to the Macready affair. On Wednesday evening "beautiful and spacious Broadway was filled in almost every department" for Forrest's rendering of *Metamora*. When Forrest appeared, "the house resounded with cheers which only ceased when their favorite commenced his part." The National, showing that "magnificent piece of stage splendor" *The Enchanter*, had a crowded house. Burton's was well filled for a farcical hodgepodge consisting of *His First Peccadillo, Herr Nanny,*

and *The Toodles*. Campbell's and Christy's Minstrels and
the Microcosmic Views were also well attended. Only the
Astor Place Opera House had a thin house. After Macready
had consented to continue his engagement, the management
decided that the theatre should not be left dark for another
night and brought out a production of *The Merry Wives of
Windsor,* with James H. Hackett, on Wednesday, May 9.
There was no hint of any disturbance at this performance,
and the *Herald* reporter was "convinced that a brilliant season is in store for this theatre."

Thirty-one Killed

Undoubtedly none of the newspaper editors wished to provoke a further disturbance on Thursday night (May 10), but their extensive publicizing of the Macready-Forrest affair on the same day and the preceding days certainly added fuel to the fires. The *Herald* printed the Macready *Replies* in their entirety. The *Daily Tribune* ran a summary of the same documents concluding with a pro-Macready sentiment: "This exposé will leave a much better impression than the injudicious violence of epithet in which Mr. Forrest has indulged!"

The *Morning Express* editorialized: "We trust that,

taught by the experiences of the past, the municipal authorities will consult at once their own credit and the claims of their constituents to be protected in the enjoyment of their rights, by taking care, beforehand, that no such outrage as that perpetrated at this establishment, last Monday night, can possibly be repeated. The managers, too, will be held responsible, this time, by public opinion, for the preservation of order. A city paper, noticing the riot of Monday night, suggests that no small portion of the blame should attach to them; as, by the indiscriminate and lavish sale of tickets, the house was so densely packed in some parts, that the police had no access to the midst of the mob, and no room to work in, if they had."

The *Express* suggested that Forrest's reputation had been injured by the violent partisanship of his followers. "We do not know what Mr. Forrest had directly to do with the matter, but it was said to be connected and consummated by persons professing to be his friends, but who, in thus attaching themselves to his quarrel, have done him more injury than all the criticism of John Forster." Nevertheless, in spite of all the unpleasantness of the preceding Monday night, it was hoped and believed that "no circumstances will hereafter occur to render so much as an allusion to it, on our part, necessary."

The *Evening Post* was the only newspaper that made any strong attempt to defend Forrest. Having already attacked the accusations against him that had been published by the *Courier and Enquirer,* the *Post* added a further comment under the heading "Another 'Fact' Retracted":

The article which we copied yesterday from the *Courier,* intended as a retraction of the charge made against Mr. Forrest, contained one assertion which has given occasion to the subjoined letter:—

No. 56 WALL ST., May 9, 1849

To the Proprietor of the *MORNING COURIER*
and *NEW YORK ENQUIRER:*—

Your article in the *Courier* of this morning has been examined by Mr. Forrest with every disposition to accept any satis-
facory withdrawal of the charges. But your paper of this
morning contains an assertion which Mr. Forrest cannot, for a
moment, allow to pass uncontradicted.

You state "as a fact" that Mr. Forrest *"had declared in public
that Mr. Macready should never be permitted to appear again
upon the stage in this city,"* and the inference again said to "be
warranted by the fact, is, that the disturbance on Monday night
was of Mr. Forrest's procurement."

Mr. Forrest pronounces this assertion to be absolutely false;
and I am instructed to request that you will at once contradict
it or give the authority on whose information the statement is
made.

I am respectfully, Your ob't serv't,
THEODORE SEDGWICK.

In publishing this note, the *Courier* says:—"It will be seen that
Mr. Forrest denies having ever declared in public that Mr. Macready should never be permitted to appear again upon the stage
of this city! Under this denial we of course presume [they found
it hard to give up] that we were misinformed in regard to the
matter, and accordingly withdraw entirely the inference drawn
from the alleged statement. We cheerfully [?] publish Mr. Sedgwick's letter, and can only renew the expression of regret that the
original statement should have been made."

The *Post* insisted, however, that "the fullest and most effectual arrangements must be made for the preservation of
order this evening" and, unlike the other papers, took a
realistic view of the evening's dangers. If no arrests were
made on Monday, "the Chief of Police had been guilty of a

culpable remissness. There were men engaged in these disturbances of sufficient notoriety to allow them to be marked and taken into custody as soon as the Police officers could get at them. It is now said that their impunity on that occasion has emboldened them to make arrangements for repeating the same acts of violence tonight in expectation of the same forbearance. If matters are not so ordered to undeceive them most thoroughly in this respect, it will be time to call for a reform of our police."

The events of May 10 bore out the *Post*'s apprehensions about the temper of the rioters. Early in the day inflammatory handbills appeared on blank walls throughout the city:

WORKINGMEN

SHALL

AMERICANS OR ENGLISH RULE

IN THIS CITY?

The crew of the English steamer has threatened all Americans who shall dare to express their opinion this night at the English Aristocratic Opera House!!

We advocate no violence, but a free expression of opinion to all public men!

WORKINGMEN! FREEMEN!!

STAND BY YOUR

LAWFUL RIGHTS.

American Committee.

This "American Committee" was headed by the notorious E. Z. C. Judson ("Ned Buntline"), publisher of "Ned Buntline's Own," a weekly "story paper" which he had started in 1848. As a writer, he is best known for his series of novels dealing with the adventures of "Buffalo Bill," an epithet which he invented in 1869 for W. F. Cody. Judson was also a sportsman, a traveler, the "hero" of a hundred fights, and a fervent advocate of "America for Americans."

It was natural enough that considerable support for the anti-Macready forces should have been drawn from the many "nativist" societies that were flourishing in the first half of the century. The earliest progenitor of these societies was the Protestant Association, founded in 1834. This group, limited at first to those with strong anti-Catholic sentiments, was quickly extended to include all who were anti-Irish. With nativist feeling still running high, however, the need for an organization with a more comprehensive doctrine was inevitably felt. As a result, in July, 1835, the Native American Democratic Association was formed. This society resolved that "We as Americans will never consent to allow the government established by our Revolutionary forefathers to pass into the hands of foreigners, and that while we open the door to the oppressed of every nation and offer a home and an asylum, we reserve the right of administering the government in conformity with the principles laid down by those who have committed it to our care." The official party organ of the Native American Democratic Association was the *Spirit of '76*.

Although no other associations were formed until 1844, nativist sentiments were becoming increasingly strong and pervasive. Two new groups were organized in 1844, the Native Sons of America and the American Brotherhood; and in 1845 another was added, the Native American Party. There were other smaller and more secretive societies such as the Patriotic Order of Sons of America, of which Judson was a member; but the strongest group was the American Brotherhood, to which he also belonged. In 1845 the Brotherhood changed its name to the Order of United Americans, which was soon shortened to O. U. A. The officers were given American Indian titles, such as Sachem for the president, and the membership was pledged to vote only for native-born citizens and to combat Catholics and foreigners whenever the occasion offered. The O. U. A. also advocated a twenty-one year probationary period before naturalization. Although extending beyond the limits of the present story, it is of interest that the organization changed its name again, in 1853, to The Supreme Order of the Star-Spangled Banner and then became generally known as the Know-Nothing party. The phrase was, of course, originated by Judson. Any member of the party who was asked about his affiliation or his political views was supposed to reply, "I know nothing" or "I don't know."

For a man like Judson (one of his admirers referred to him as a "modern knight errant") the troubles that followed upon the feud between Forrest and Macready presented a glorious opportunity to advance the doctrine of "America for Americans." Furthermore Judson had been under fire from James Gordon Bennett's *Herald* for a slanderous attack on Bennett's sister, and Bennett, like Macready, was a Britisher. The theatre managers, Hackett and Niblo, were also open to suspicion. Hackett was a "broken-down aristocrat," and Niblo was an Irishman. Here, decidedly, was Ned Buntline's chance to do his bit.

According to the report of his wife, he put in a busy day on May 10: "Ned in blue frock coat with gilt buttons and tall hat, drove furiously around town in a light wagon soliciting support. In the evening he put on a short, light-colored 'monkey-jacket' and Tom Hyer cap, ideal for action as well as disguise."

After the morning's rehearsal at the Opera House—at which, it was reported, there was "no apprehension among the company"—the management had all the windows "which fronted the streets, and which communicated with the audience and with the persons attached to the theatre" carefully barricaded with inch and a half boards. The Mayor meanwhile had ordered the city's cleaning detail to cart away all the paving stones "which had been raised for the purpose of constructing a sewer in the vicinity." Unfortunately these instructions were not very carefully followed.

At 11:00 A.M. Mayor Caleb S. Woodhull called the strategy council already alluded to. What an unhappy beginning for the new Mayor, his second day in office! At the Coroner's Inquest two days later Woodhull gave his full account of this meeting.

I was informed that there was likely to be a disturbance at the theatre in Astor-place on the evening of May 10; I sent for the Recorder and several gentlemen to be at my office at 11 o'clock; Recorder Tallmadge; J. J. V. Westervelt, Sheriff; the Chief of Police, G. W. Matsell; General Sandford, the Police Justices and Mr. Niblo all came; Mr. Hackett came with Mr. Niblo; I inquired of Mr. Niblo, the proprietor of the theatre, whether they were going to perform that night; he replied that they had put out their bill, and proposed to do so; I then inquired of the gentlemen present what the probabilities were that there would be a disturbance. The Chief of Police said that he thought it might be serious; conversation then passed between those present on the subject and the means to be used to suppress any disturbance then talked of. I inquired of the Chief of Police whether the civil force would be sufficient; he said that he thought it would not. I then asked him if he thought the military would be required; he said that he thought it would. I then put the question to each person individually, whether, under the circumstances, an order should be issued; they all answered in the affirmative, except General Sandford. General Hall was not present. General Sandford said that it was not his business to advise on the subject, but it was his business to obey the order if one was issued. The order was issued and delivered to General Sandford's son. The order was a general one; the number to be called out was left to General Sandford. Some conversation was had between myself, Mr. Niblo and Mr. Hackett upon the subject of closing the theatre; I stated to Mr. Niblo, that as a Magistrate I had no authority to interfere with his establishment, but my private wishes were, that he should close his theatre on that night. They seemed to think that they ought not to close their theatre, but that the Magistracy should protect them. We then came to the conclusion that their house should be protected. Instructions were then given to the Chief of Police and to General Sandford to take such measures as the case might require. Nothing further occurred through the day, except the details to carry out the instructions that had been given.

General Sandford, in his testimony, agreed with the Mayor's version of the meeting but added these details.

It was understood by the magistrates present, that the effort should be made by the civil authority to preserve the peace; and that the military should not be called out until that effort failed. I received in consequence, the following order, after I left the Mayor's office:

MAYOR'S OFFICE, CITY HALL, May 10, 1849

Having reason to apprehend a serious riot this evening, which will require more force to preserve the peace than is possessed by the police, Major General Sandford is requested to hold a sufficient military force in readiness to meet the apprehended emergency.

C. W. WOODHULL, *Mayor*

Frederick A. Tallmadge, the Recorder (he was the first in New York to be elected by popular vote), added only one item to the Mayor's account of the conference. He had informed Messrs. Niblo and Hackett "that he feared if there

DETAIL OF ASTOR PLACE RIOT

was a performance they would sustain serious injury to their house, and if they insisted upon a performance the county could not be responsible for the injury they might sustain."

The stage was set for the big event, both inside and out-side the Opera House. The script was still to be written, but the scenario was in order, and the *dramatis personae* had been determined. Shortly after mid-afternoon of Thursday, May 10, the members of the cast began to take their places.

At four o'clock in the afternoon George W. Matsell, Chief of Police, went to the Opera House with the officers of his force to make the necessary arrangements. Just before six o'clock his three hundred twenty-five policemen (thirteen platoons) arrived. Two hundred were stationed in different parts of the theatre to preserve order. Fifty covered the rear of the building along Eighth Street, and the remaining seventy-five surrounded the house and stables on the southwest corner of Astor Place and Lafayette, opposite the main entrance of the theatre. The house and stables belonged to Mrs. Walter Langdon, the youngest daughter of the first John Jacob Astor. Although the main building was occupied by someone at the time of the riot, it is not clear where Mrs. Langdon was.

While the police were assuming their positions at the Opera House, the military were gathering at their assembly points farther downtown. General Sandford had ordered out the Seventh Regiment, commonly known to the public as the National Guards, under the command of Colonel Duryea. This regiment consisted of eight companies "numbering three or four hundred men, on parade; but as the notice was short and late in the day, they numbered only a little over two hundred at mustering." These companies, led by Captains Shumway, Underhill, Pond, and Price, assem-

bled at the Artillery Drill Room at Centre Market and received their ammunition—fifteen hundred rounds of ball
cartridges.

Two troops of horse, led by Captains Varnum and Patter-
son and under the command of General Hall, mustered at
the Arsenal along with one troop of light artillery. Two six-
pound cannons were given to the artillery with a supply of
grape and canister shot, and a small detachment of infantry
was assigned to protect the pieces. Two companies of hussars
attached to General George P. Morris's Brigade were also
ordered to wait in readiness. At 7:30 General Sandford sent
word to the magistrates at the Opera House that his military forces were prepared and would await their orders.

All during the day there had been a rush for tickets, and
before the doors were opened, at seven o'clock, the number
of tickets sold exceeded the theatre's capacity of 1,800. When
Macready arrived at the Opera House, at twenty minutes to
six, Astor Place was already filling with people. With the
memory of Monday night still vividly in his mind, he was
comforted to see so many policemen already on duty. The
main doors to the theatre were strongly protected by a hollow square of policemen, "the entrance to which was
through a double file of the same."

By 7:15, fifteen minutes before curtain time, Astor Place
from Broadway to the Bowery was packed almost solid.
Overcast skies and a temperature in the low fifties were evidently no deterrents. There was such a tremendous crush
about the theatre doors, in spite of the posted notice stating
that all tickets had been sold, that the entrances were barred
and police details stationed in front of them. Evidently not
all the ticket holders had been admitted when the doors
were closed, for the house was not filled. But it was crowded
with police. All the lobbies, the staircases, and the lower

rooms were lined with "stars." They were stationed in squads throughout the parquet, balcony, and boxes; in the second tier a line stretched all around the house between the front and back row of boxes; and a large detachment was posted in the amphitheatre.

In spite of the rough appearance of many of the spectators and the almost total absence of women—there seem to have been only seven—the general behavior of the audience was, for the moment, surprisingly respectable and quiet. The curtain rose about ten minutes late, and the first two scenes went off without incident. On his first entrance a vociferous welcome was given to Mr. Clarke, who, as on Monday, was playing Macduff. But when Macready entered in the third scene, a storm of cheers, groans, and hisses broke loose. The "nine-tenths" of the audience that were friendly to Macready rose and applauded, waving their hats and handkerchiefs, but their numbers were no match for the energy and violence of their opponents. The tumult lasted for fifteen minutes during which the stage action stopped completely. Finally the management pushed in a board from the wings which read, "The friends of Order will remain quiet." This silenced Macready's supporters but not the rioters; although the play proceeded, not a word from the stage could be heard by anyone. Evidently the police were awaiting specific orders, for during this initial protest no attempt was made to deter the rioters. The civil authorities, still hoping that the mere presence of the police would check the would-be rioters, had decided to do nothing for the time being.

The Mayor did not arrive at the Opera House until nine o'clock, but Recorder Tallmadge had gotten there at 7:30 and, finding a "multitude of people collected" passed among them and mingled with them, it then being still light enough

to discern people." Even after the doors were closed he
stayed outside the building.

Inside, Chief of Police Matsell was attended by Sidney
Stuart (Clerk of the Police at the Halls of Justice), Justice
McGrath, Judge Edmonds, and Sheriff Westervelt. Matsell
had informed his subordinates that no move was to be made
except by his direction, though the men were to "talk to the
people at every opportunity and persuade them to be quiet."
No arrests were going to be made "unless for some actual
overt act tending absolutely to a breach of the public peace;
with a reasonable indulgence they might hiss or applaud
consistent with the maintenance of the public order." The
Chief stationed himself in the Astor House box on the right
of the stage, where he could be clearly seen in the event that
he had any orders to give. When the demonstration began,
Stuart asked the Chief if the time had not arrived to begin
the arrests. Matsell hesitated, but "finally sent me for the
Recorder to consult as to the propriety of making the arrest." Stuart found the Recorder still outside the building
and brought him to the Chief. Matsell took Tallmadge to
the north (Eighth Street) side of the theatre and pointed
out several disorderly persons who were threatening to attack Macready. Tallmadge immediately ordered their arrest.
Finally, in the last scene of the first act, Matsell "made his
appearance in the parquette, and, followed by three or four
gigantic fellows, marched directly down the aisle to the
leader of the disturbance, whom he secured after a short but
violent struggle in which the rioters were nearly stripped of
their clothing. One by one the rowdies were taken and carried out, the greater part of the audience applauding as they
disappeared." The Recorder believed that by making two or
three arrests "the tumult would be quelled." During the

intermission those arrested were secured in a room below the parquet.

When the second act began, the lower part of the house was indeed quieter, but the upper tiers renewed their attack with increased force. One of the demonstrators managed to poke his head through a barricaded upper window to advise those outside that some of their friends had been placed under arrest. At the same time a policeman thrust a hose pipe through one of the lower windows and began to spray water on the mob. Whether from these actions or just from the growing tension of the crowd outside, the attack on the building now began.

A *Tribune* reporter, on May 11, gave the following account of this second act debacle as it appeared from outside the theatre. "As one window after another cracked, the pieces of bricks and paving-stones rattled in on the terraces and lobbies, the confusion increased, till the Opera House resembled a fortress besieged by an invading army rather than a place meant for the peaceful amusement of a civilized community. Sometimes heavy stones would dash in the boards which had been nailed up as protection, and a number of policemen were constantly occupied in nailing up and securing the defenses. The attack was sometimes on one side and sometimes on the other, but seemed to be most violent on Eighth Street where there was a continual volley of stones and other missiles. The retiring-rooms were closed, and the lobbies so 'raked' by the mob outside, that the only safe places were the boxes and the parquette. A stone, thrown through an upper window, took effect upon the magnificent chandelier hanging in the centre of the theatre and ruined it." And through all of this "the obnoxious actor went through his part with perfect self-possession, and paid no regard to the tumultuous scene before him."

The *Courier and Enquirer* (May 12) observer supplied
some additional details. "Stones came thick and fast through
the windows, being of such size and thrown with such force
that the heavy plank barricades were frequently driven in,
and were obliged to be replaced by the officers and carpenters in attendance. A plank was driven off with such force
that it shot, end first, across the passage way known as 'fop's
alley,' across the balcony, and was falling into the pit, where
it would have injured many, when it struck the balustrade
and was secured. Through the upper windows the stones
flew freely, many of them weighing three and four pounds.
We have one such in our possession which struck the box
just behind the head of a gentleman in the 2nd tier. Had its
aim been a few inches higher his head would have been
severely injured."

The main action now shifted. The demonstrators inside
had been subdued, but the attack from the outside prompted
the Recorder to rush out to the street and order the police to
arrest anyone who was seen throwing a stone.

The first major action occurred on the Eighth Street side
of the theatre. The police were driven back against the wall
of the building, and heavy stones were aimed at the doors,
nearly breaking them down. The Sheriff, who had ventured
out onto Astor Place (on the south side) came back into the
theatre and rallied a platoon of policemen to reinforce the
Eighth Street side. They opened the large door of the building and, rushing against the crowd, managed to drive back
those in the first ranks. Most of the attackers seem to have
been boys from fifteen to seventeen. Six to ten of these were
arrested and brought into the house. The arrests were not
easily managed, for immediately the police had their hands
on a man, his friends would attempt to rescue him.

Now, as the crowd tried to storm the main entrance, the

pressure turned to the Astor Place side of the building. The mob here was becoming more dense and excited, "exhibiting a disposition to do something," though the participants again were mostly boys, the older and larger portion of the crowd apparently consisting of spectators.

Policeman William McKinney of the Thirteenth Ward described this stage of the action as follows:

> We were beaten from the door, not into the theatre, but from it, so that the crowd was between us and the door. We were at the curbstone. Before we were driven to the curb the stones hit us; whether they were thrown at us or at the door I cannot say. Afterwards they went over our heads.
>
> I was knocked down myself. I endeavored to arrest one of the men who was killed [*sic*], previous to the arrival of the military, but he was taken away from me, and I was dragged across the street to the curbstone. This man, after he was killed, was taken inside into the opera house. He was shot. I saw him inside. He was throwing a stone when I arrested him.

This man was Thomas Kiernan. Whether his death occurred before or after the military arrived is not clear (McKinney's later testimony on this point is confused), but there is no doubt that Kiernan was the first fatality. He was twenty-one years old, he had been born in Ireland, and he was a waiter. He had been living at 196 East Thirteenth Street and, according to Bernard Manning, a fellow boarder at that address, was "an honest, sober, and steady man."

As the stoning continued, more and more policemen were injured and carried into the Opera House. Benjamin P. Fairchild, Captain of the Eighth Ward Police, had been assigned by Chief Matsell to follow the activities outside the building and keep him informed. According to Fairchild's report, "About 8 o'clock I reported to the Chief that I thought it would be impossible to retain our position much

longer, as the lines had been broken. I was directed to rally
the men and make another effort. There was a space cleared
in front of the theatre, the people having left to avoid the
stones. After this I went again on the 8th street side, and
found one or two hundred young men and boys stoning the
building. I attempted to make an arrest of one and was
beaten back by the mob and had to run for my life. After
finding that the line had been broken up, I went to the Astor
Place side, I got inside with difficulty. I found the Chief, the
Recorder, and the Sheriff, I reported to them that I thought
it was impossible for the police to keep the crowd back—
that they would demolish the building unless we were reinforced."

At the same time, the Recorder was hurrying "to the eastern part of the Opera House, where there was a severe pressure on the police, which became so severe on the Bowery
side that the police were driven in. It was utterly impossible
to resist. They were, as well as the building, assailed with
stones; three of them fell by my [Tallmadge's] side. I was
struck myself several times, but not severely. I found it was
impossible for the civil force to resist. The mob had approached so near the main entrance of the theatre that they
commenced breaking in the doors with large stones. I rushed
into the house, finding that the police had been overcome
and could not resist, for the purpose of seeing the Sheriff, to
have the military ordered."

The Sheriff, the Recorder, and the Chief of Police consulted inside the theatre and agreed that the military must
be sent for. The verbal order was given by the Sheriff to one
of his deputies, who immediately carried the message down
Broadway to the Artillery Rooms. The Recorder then ordered all the police to rally inside the Opera House and to
hold possession of the building until the military arrived.

Some twenty policemen had already been injured, and he did not wish to risk any further casualties in a vain attempt to beat back the attackers.

These accounts by the civil authorities are unquestionably more accurate than the more circumstantial reports of some of the eyewitnesses in the crowd, who seem to have underrated what was happening or to have seen it incompletely. Stephen Gaines, of 30 Broadway, reported that he was at the corner of Lafayette Place and Astor Place, having arrived there about a quarter past eight o'clock.

I was within a picket enclosure and stood upon a pile of boards that were within a foot of the top of the fence; I remained there until after the last discharge of musketry. From the place where I stood I had a fair view of the Opera House, which was on the opposite side of the street towards Broadway. I saw persons throwing stones at the windows and principal entrance of the Opera House, sometimes a single stone and at other times volleys were thrown principally at the windows above the principal entrance. There were so few engaged in actually storming the house, that surprise was several times expressed by the spectators about me that it was permitted, and that the police did not stop it.

Dennis Ryer, a former policeman, said that he was standing on the sidewalk at Mrs. Langdon's house. "I saw some boys and a few men throwing stones, first at the street lamps in front of the theatre, then at the windows of the theatre."

Certainly the twenty bruised-up policemen would not have agreed with these descriptions of the attack. They and their frightened cohorts were happy to remain in the comparative safety of the interior of the building while they waited for the military. There were some doubts as to whether the Opera House could withstand the siege, but when these doubts were strengthened by the strong smell of smoke that began to permeate the building, the situation really began to appear hopeless. Here were all the civil authorities stranded in a building which they could neither leave nor occupy without peril to their lives. Fortunately, however, the fire, which was discovered under the parquet, was quickly and easily put out. The alarm did not reach panic proportions.

Samuel Alberti, police officer of the Fifteenth Ward, had been left in charge of the prisoners who had been first taken into custody. These five men, William Sparks, Robert Bennett, Charles Tappen, Robert Miller, and James McLean, had been locked in a small room under the parquet. Alberti had handcuffed Miller and McLean together because they had threatened to set the building on fire if he did not release them. Alberti ignored their threats, locked the door, and took his station outside. Inside the room the men gathered a bundle of shavings and ignited them with a "gas lamp which had been improperly left burning in the room they occupied, with the horrible intention of destroying the building and its occupants."

Around nine o'clock, just after the beginning of the third act—the play was continuing in spite of everything—the military arrived. And just as the soldiers were turning into Astor Place, the Mayor appeared on the scene.

I made myself known at the door, and went into the house; I enquired of the Recorder, Chief of Police, and Sheriff, what they were doing. The general answer was, there was a large force outside; they stated that the windows and panels of the doors were broken in; the military were outside. It was stated by the Chief of Police that great difficulty was to be entertained as to keeping them from breaking into the house, with the force he had, and he was fearful they would succeed, as his men were doing all they could do. After I had been there about fifteen minutes, General Hall stated to me that unless I gave orders for his men to fire, his men would leave the ground; my answer was, not yet, General, let us see; he said he had been struck with stones on his head and body, and the blood at this time was running down the left side of his face; he repeated twice or three times that his men would not stand to be stoned to death with arms in their hands; finally he stated to me, Mayor, you must give the order to fire, or my men will all be killed; my answer was again, "wait a little." Nothing passed again between the General and myself; he left me without the order. I did not give the order to fire. There was no proclamation read to the people by me; I was inside. There was no proclamation issued by me that day. I issued none, because I was not sufficiently informed of the state of facts to deem it necessary; the means taken through the day were precautionary. About twenty minutes after General Hall left me, I notified Justice Mountfort that I was going to the New York Hotel, and should remain there to receive any communication they had to make; I then left, in company with my brother, and went to the New York Hotel. This was previous to the firing of the military. I remained at the Hotel with Governor [Hamilton] Fish until after eleven o'clock, and then went to my house; the disturbance then appeared to be over.

This was the account that Woodhull gave to the Coroner's Jury. Obviously the Mayor recognized the seriousness of the events. A true politician, though only two days in office, he saw the danger involved in any active participation. Clearly the best course was to get off the premises as rapidly as possible and leave the decisions to subordinates.

On receiving the request for military assistance, General Sandford had sent orders to the Arsenal Yard: the "horse belonging to this regiment, and a small number of horse of another regiment assembled there, [were] to come in front of the drill rooms and march to the ground. There was no ammunition given to the horse; they had nothing but their

ASTOR PLACE RIOT: THE LAST VOLLEY

sabres." Brigadier General Hall, of the First Division of the Thirtieth Brigade, proceeded at the right of the infantry, and General Sandford took the right of the cavalry. The troops were put under march and moved rapidly up Broadway to Astor Place, General Sandford and his cavalry of fifty horsemen in the lead.

The procession seems to have been noticeably deficient in military bearing. According to one observer, "Had they understood their business and been well mounted the streets might have been cleared without bloodshed. They consisted principally of milkmen and carmen; persons belonging to those classes usually joining that arm of the service, from the circumstance that they can ride their own horses when required to parade, while other citizens would be obliged, on such occasions to hire the animals, they made use of." But these uniformed soldiers—however ununiform they might have appeared—were the best that could be had for the maintenance of law and order.

When the forces arrived at the corner of Broadway and Astor Place, the infantry halted while Sandford directed his cavalry to form a front of ten men and to wheel right and proceed into Astor Place. The press of the crowd was so great that it took the cavalry about twenty minutes to cover the hundred feet to the front entrance of the theatre and clear a path along which the infantry might move. Perceiving the difficulty of the horsemen, General Hall cautioned his men "not to show any resentment" no matter what abuses were hurled at them and then ordered them to move forward with "fixed bayonets."

At first the militia were "saluted only with groans, hisses and insults," but when they tried to force their way on past the Opera House, they were assailed by stones and brickbats. According to General Sandford, "every man was more or less hurt and the horses were rendered almost unmanageable. A dense mob extended as far as I could see to the Third Avenue. The mounted men, being conspicuous marks, received most of the stones, and were finally driven off the ground. I dismounted, returned through the mob, and took charge of the infantry, who were halted in line across the open space beyond the theatre, with a dense mob on both sides, who were assailing them with all sorts of opprobrious epithets and frequent volleys of stones. I ordered General Hall and Colonel Duryea to form a column of divisions and move forward."

When the troops got beyond the theatre and into the open square facing the Bowery, the men requested that General Hall give an order to prime and load. "I hesitated some time, knowing that every cartridge we had was a ball cartridge." Not being able to locate General Sandford for further specific orders, Hall ordered his men to form a hollow square, opposite the Opera House, and with what remained of the "troops of horse on the flanks of the square." While halted in this position, the soldiers were continually assaulted by stones. Hall himself was struck several times.

In a few moments General Sandford came up and ordered the men to proceed west along Eighth Street toward Broadway in an effort to clear the street at the rear (the north side) of the theatre. They pushed forward through the mob "until stopped by an excavation in the ground, which was not seen, owing to the darkness of the night." The excavation was bypassed, and the troops took up positions behind the Opera House, at the center of the building. They were ordered to line up in two units, four deep, one facing west toward Broadway and the other east toward the Bowery. These two units pushed forward simultaneously in opposite directions, cleared the entire street of rioters, and stationed themselves at the two ends of the Opera House on Eighth Street.

General Hall then went into the theatre to see the Mayor. He informed him that it was impossible "to maintain our position without the assistance of a magistrate, as many of our men were knocked down and seriously hurt." Sheriff Westervelt and Chief of Police Matsell left the building with Hall and went with him to confer with General Sandford. Sandford told Matsell that a detachment of policemen was needed to take over the positions held by the military so that the latter could try to clear the area in front of the theatre. The police were called out of the building and were required to replace the soldiers across the two ends of Eighth Street. The troops—accompanied, at Sandford's request, by the Sheriff—marched along Eighth Street toward Broadway, turned south on Broadway, and then proceeded into Astor Place. Because of the density of the mob there, the soldiers were obliged to file along the sidewalk next to the building until they reached the main entrance.

General Sandford's intention was to perform the same maneuver that he had managed in Eighth Street. The troops were formed four deep and ordered to force their way across Astor Place. After getting about two thirds of the way across, they were forced back by showers of paving stones. Many who were knocked down were carried by the police into the Opera House. The rest retreated to the sidewalk and formed ranks again. It was in this area that the pavement had been broken up for the purpose of laying water pipes and building a sewer, so the mob was well supplied with ammunition.

After the troops had re-formed, General Sandford ordered them to try again to force their way across the street. The regiment was then to be divided into two wings, one to advance east toward the Bowery and the other west toward

Broadway; thus the mob was to be driven from the area in front of the theatre on Astor Place. General Sandford gave his own account of the attempted maneuver:

After giving this order, I advanced myself toward the middle of the street, by the side of Captain Shumway, who led the first company, and Colonel Duryea, who was by his side, I being on the outside next the mob. The Sheriff was just behind me. When we were nearly two-thirds of the way across the street, we were assailed by a volley of stones, by which more than two-thirds in the front rank were more or less injured—the Captain, the Colonel and myself being struck too; eight out of eleven men constituting the front rank were more or less injured. At this time a pistol was fired by some man in the mob, within a very short distance of the troops by which Captain Shumway was wounded in the leg, as I believe, General Hall in the face, although I did not hear till afterwards; previous to this the crowd had been repeatedly notified by General Hall and myself, and by other persons, whose voices I did not recognize, that they must disperse or they would be fired upon; I was partly knocked down at this time, and when I rose, found three or four of the front rank down likewise, and the head of the column forced back towards the Opera House; the shower of stones being at this time incessant, orders were then given by myself and repeated by Colonel Duryea, to charge bayonets; the attempt was made, but the mob was so close upon the troops pressing upon them, that there was no room for the troops to charge, and some of the men had their muskets seized by the crowd.

General Hall's version of this stage of the action recorded similar frustrations.

Some of the mob attempted to wrest the pieces from the hands of the military, but could not succeed; I tried to form a line, but was only able to succeed partially; some person said to me, "Why don't you fire?" I cannot say who it was; I think it was the Chief of Police; I made the remark that we had no right to fire on an occasion like this unless we had an order from the magistrates; several of my men on both sides were knocked down; at this time General Sandford was some twelve feet from me, partially down. At this time I was on the right of the column; the Recorder was near by; the Colonel on my left; one of the men who had been knocked down was badly hurt, said it was too bad to be hurt, and "not be able to prevent it," Colonel Duryea made the remark, "Never mind, boys, stick to your guns"; some person, I think the Recorder exhorted the mob to disperse, or if they did not the military would fire; the noise and confusion was so great that I don't think it was heard ten feet from where I stood; one of the men had his bayonet knocked from his gun, and the rattling of stones against the guns tended to increase the noise; one of the men had his gun rendered useless by a stone striking it with so much force as to bend the pan across the barrel; at this time more than thirty of our men were disabled.

The troops were again forced back to the sidewalk. Captain Pond, in command of the company holding the position directly in front of the theatre entrance, was hit with a stone and "taken off the ground"; and the next officer in line took over and advised General Sandford that if the men did not get orders to fire, they would have to abandon the streets. Sandford passed this word along to Sheriff Westervelt, who had to make the final decision, the Mayor having already left the premises. Westervelt agreed that the moment demanded drastic action, but he felt that the crowd must be given warning before a single shot were fired. He and the Recorder then went among the mob expostulating with them and cautioning them that they would be fired upon if they did not desist. In the noise and confusion very little was heard, and what was heard was ignored. The Sheriff returned to the line of soldiers now backed up against the building and gave Hall permission to fire, requesting, however, that the guns be aimed over the heads of the rioters.

The Recorder, who had disappeared into the crowd, was not with the military when this order was given. Chief of Police Matsell advised Hall to hold off for a while and "give them the cold steel, they'll fear that more than the lead"; but Hall proceeded to give the "ready" order, which was announced by Colonel Duryea and General Sandford. Hall then stepped in front of the troops and directed them to elevate their pieces and aim at the house (Mrs. Langdon's house) across the street—between the first and second stories. The men fired when ordered to, and the musket balls banged against the wall, then dropped to the ground as "flat as pancakes." This first order to fire was given about three quarters of an hour after the soldiers had entered Astor Place.

General Hall has left his account of what happened just before this first volley.

While standing there, a stone struck me in the small of the back and knocked the breath out of me, and made me stagger, the effects of which I have felt ever since. I looked immediately on the right of the column, and about this time, at any rate before we had fired, some of the men told me that Captain Shumway, Eighth Company, National Guards, was badly hurt in the leg, though we were not at that time aware that it was by a shot; he remained with me until he found the blood running into his boot so as to make his foot very wet; after we had fired he went into the Opera House. I was also told that my cheek was bleeding; I had not felt any stone or pain more than like the prick of a pin; at home, however, a small hole was found in my cheek, a little larger than the head of a pin; my cheek bled for more than two hours.

The sound of gunfire frightened the crowd into an immediate but short-lived retreat. Someone yelled out that the soldiers were firing blank cartridges, and a number of others took up the chorus: "They've got leather flints and blank cartridges." The mob became more infuriated than before, "commenced wresting the muskets from the soldiers' hands," and "pelting stones as large as your double fist like a shower of hail."

At this moment the Recorder, according to his report, "rushed out into the mob and invoked them to depart, as the military would fire directly upon them. The Sheriff, and Mr. Charles Duane, commonly called 'Dutch Charley' (who, I must say, did his duty nobly) accompanied me to the curb-stone. While urging the mob to disperse, I was assailed by a volley of stones, and was injured on my ankle and other parts of my body and was forced to retreat into the rear of the military."

The rowdies were now in no temper to listen to speeches. As one reporter described them, "They came from an element of the community that, ungovernable in itself, knowing no law and having nothing at stake, is always ready to lend itself to mischief, for the mere sake of seeing how easily it can work mischief." The description may have been too simple, but there is certainly no doubt that the Recorder's pleas for law and order were as ineffective as his threats. One man, "a grimed and burly ruffian with a huge stone between his knees, exposing with both hands his bare breast covered with a red flannel shirt, cried: 'Fire into this. Take the life out of a free-born American for a bloody British actor! Do it, Ay, You darsn't.'" Some of the rioters, said to have been clothed in firemen's uniforms and equipped with scaling ladders, were shouting: "Burn the damned den of the aristocracy!" One orator explained, "You can't go in there without kid gloves on. I paid for a ticket, and they would not let me in, because I hadn't kid gloves and a white vest, damn 'em!" Someone else, a more temperate soul, was able to "luxuriate in the scene." "Hurrah!" he shouted, "I will have nothing to do with breaking windows, but I luxuriate in the scene." Ned Buntline was parading in front of the crowd, swinging his sword and asking loudly, "Workingmen, shall Americans or English rule? Shall the sons whose fathers drove the baseborn miscreants from the shores give up their Liberty!"

When the Recorder returned, Sheriff Westervelt instructed General Hall to fire again. Hall shouted to his men to "fire low, so as not to hit above the legs; if blood was to be spilt, we were in hopes that life would not be taken." According to Hall, he—and General Sandford and Colonel Duryea—had to repeat the order three times before the troops fired. "The hallooing, screaming, and shouting was so great that it was impossible for the third file, thirty feet away from me, to hear what was said." Although the soldiers had earlier pleaded to be permitted to defend themselves, they were now horror-stricken at the idea of firing directly at their fellow citizens.

The troops next moved forward across Astor Place, driving the crowd before them into Lafayette Place and toward the Bowery. One group of rioters rallied on the south side of Astor Place at the Lafayette Place corner and another group on the stretch of broken ground (east of the theatre) where the paving stones had been left. The soldiers, now facing toward the Bowery, were treated to another bombardment. At the same time their strength was gradually diminishing as more of them were struck and carried into the Opera House. The Recorder informed Hall that they would have to fire again, and Hall asked the Recorder to try again to persuade the mob to disperse. "The Recorder and some others whom I do not recollect went—the Recorder requested we would not fire until they should return; to which

I replied, there was no danger, we should not fire if we could help it, at all events, not until they returned. They returned in a very few moments, being assailed with a continuous hail of stones."

The order to fire was given again, half the troops aiming obliquely to the right at the group gathered in Lafayette Place and the other half to the left at those who were holding to the southeast corner of the theatre. The crowd fell back beyond the patch of broken pavement, in the direction of the Bowery, still managing, however, to lob stones and brickbats through the air. The additional discharge of gunfire was the last for the night, but there is disagreement about the total number of volleys fired. General Hall, who should have been in a position to know, said that there were "four distinct firings," whereas General Sandford and Sheriff Westervelt could account for only three.

Except for this discrepancy, the reports of the officials are probably accurate in their description of the movements of the military, but the specific instances of violence—which sometimes happened with a kind of tragicomic abruptness and incongruity—are more circumstantially reported in the eyewitness accounts provided by some of the "innocent" bystanders and by some of the policemen who were carrying the wounded into the Opera House. There is, in the unofficial reports, a wealth of detail which conveys a good deal of the confusion and general miscellaneousness of events.

Thomas J. Veldren, a boatman, who stationed himself at the corner of Mrs. Langdon's house, reported:

I got there about half past 6 o'clock; a few began to throw stones, but carts and omnibusses had no hesitation in passing through; those throwing stones were half grown boys. I stood on the southeast corner of Lafayette Place and Astor Place talking to two Philadelphians about the riots there, until the military came up, when there was quite a rush by the boys, to which we gave way, but afterwards returned; I crossed over again to Mrs. Langdon's corner, being anxious to see what was going on; the crowd was then greater and more noisy, and when the military passed through they rushed back and the stoning went on again. I stood at that corner until the first volley was fired, and that was the first thing I heard because of the noise. I saw a man fall out among the people towards the corner. The people near me and I laughed. We thought it was a blank cartridge to scare them. I reached over to see what was going on, but could not see, but heard a man say, "My God, look at this!" By what I heard said I think he was shot through the breast. This was the first discharge. I then started and ran to the corner of the church down Lafayette Place. I there heard some more shots, then I started for home. I saw them carrying bodies after the last report. Was not engaged in the riot. Went to look on. Would not have been there if I had thought they had been going to use lead.

Most of the witnesses agreed that plenty of stones were thrown—but only from the front rank by about three hundred young boys, fourteen to sixteen. One observer said that where he was the crowd was so dense "a man could not have thrown a stone if he had it in his hand." Most agreed, too, that if the military gave any order to disperse before firing, the order was not heard. Certainly it would have taken an uncommonly loud shout to be heard above the continuing racket. Nor was the order to fire above the heads of the people heard by all the soldiers who fired. Stephen Gaines, formerly a policeman, said, "I could see the discharges distinctly, as all the lamps were out. Some of them fired nearly perpendicular, some in a slanting direction towards Mrs. Langdon's house, and some horizontally. This was the first discharge; we had no intimation of their intention to fire where I stood until we saw the flash." Another insisted that in the first volley at least a quarter of the soldiers fired

horizontally and directly into the crowd. One man said he
saw a soldier fire after the rest. "He lowered his piece, and
looked at or did something to the lock and then raised it,
took deliberate aim about the height of a man's breast and
fired."

Before it was apparent that some of the crowd had been
dropped by the first volley, there was a general uproar of
"blank cartridges!" And when the Recorder passed through
the military to address the mob, "He was answered from a
great many voices—principally boys, I should say, but some
men, and it seemed like a great shout, to this purport, 'Fire
you sons of bitches, fire—you durst not fire.' From the sound
of the boys' voices, I should suppose they were about sixteen." This was the report of Charles Cook, captain of the
First Ward Police.

The stories were often painfully detailed.

Sylvester L. Wiley had gone to the Opera House at half-
past six and taken a position on the railing of Mrs. Langdon's house,

. . . where I remained until after the first discharge by the infantry. Mr. George W. Gedney was in front of me when he was
shot. He was standing on the inside of the railing looking on at
the disturbance. He had his right hand in his pocket and a cane
in the other, looking on and having nothing to say except to make
remarks on what was passing. He was killed at the first discharge
of the muskets. As soon as I saw him fall, I got off the railing inside. A gentleman then had hold of him. I took hold of his head
and found it bloody and let it go again. I went to the corner of
Lafayette Place about twenty-five feet distant, and called some
one to come help and carry out a dead man. I came back and two
men had raised him up; I laid his back upon my back with his
head and shoulders in front of me, and they carried the rest of his
body. We tried to get into Mrs. Langdon's house, as we did not

know how much he was hurt. We knocked at the door, which was opened by a gentleman, who repulsed us as soon as he saw what we wanted; he closed the door as far as he could but the crowd pressed so he could not get it quite closed, he sang out for assistance, when three or four men came from the back door, one of whom—a policeman, I knew him by his star—struck me over the head and knocked my hat off, so that it fell in the hall. I called on the crowd to give way, that we could not get in there; as soon as we could get off we took him to the Fifteenth Ward Station House, where he lay until past 12 o'clock before he was recognized.

John Clarke, a bookbinder, was also in front of the Langdon house. "After the first firing a man fell nearly in front of me; some said he had a fit, and others said he was struck with a stone; we picked him up and carried him to a drug store, corner of Broadway and Eighth Street; no person believed that he had been wounded by a musket ball until they saw the wound themselves; then a good many swore vengeance and left. He was shot through the left lung. I have heard since that his name was Brown."

Stephen Gaines saw the man immediately in front of him fall.

Above half a dozen persons near him on the sidewalk at the time supposed, as did I, that he had fallen intentionally. He laid upon the ground perhaps half a minute before any person went to his assistance, and the remark was made that he was shamming shot. We did not discover whether he was really wounded or not until one who had his hands under his back felt the blood running through his fingers; we stopped at a doctor's in Fourth Street, but could not obtain admittance, and took the body to the corner of Fourth and Wooster, to a drug store. On carrying him in and opening his breast, we discovered he was wounded in his stomach, a little lower perhaps than the middle of his stomach;

his shirt was saturated with blood, and some clotted blood or a portion of the contents of his stomach. His name was ascertained to be Henry Otten, residing at the corner of Hester and Orchard. I understand he died soon afterwards at the Station House. He was not taking part in the disturbances, nor were any of those in that neighborhood. After leaving him at the druggist's, as he was preparing to sponge the wound, I first learned that others had been shot.

John B. Levrich, a varnisher and polisher of 79 East Thirteenth Street, stood nearly opposite the Astor Place entrance of the theatre.

I was not in company with any person; I went to look for a friend whom I had left a little time before. I moved a little, but not over ten feet when the military fired; one man that was leaning on my shoulder with his left hand and his cap in his right was shot in the groin in the first fire. This man after they fired, said that they were firing blank cartridges. In a minute or a minute and a half after saying this he sat down. It was the only way he could get down, the crowd was so great. I thought he had stopped to pick up a stone. I stooped to pick him up when another man was shot in the head who fell against me and covered my face with blood. As soon as I turned round I saw the military forming in line across the street and I started to run. After going a few steps I turned back and assisted in picking the men up. I assisted in carrying them as far as Langdon's corner, then so many crowded around that I let go. I did not know either of the persons shot but I saw a man that I thought was one of them lying on a billiard table at Vauxhall Gardens [a park and amusement area between Lafayette Place and the Bowery]. One man was lying on the table dead. After leaving these men I went on the north west corner of Eighth Street and the Bowery and found a man named Stewart who was lying on the sidewalk, who had been shot. Several persons were standing around him. I sat down on the curb, for it made me sick. I heard more firing, and after a

little while I went down Eighth Street towards the Opera House;
I saw some persons carrying a man who was shot in the leg.
They called to me to assist them; I endeavored to do so. We went
down Eighth Street towards Broadway, but the policemen objected to our passing. After a little while however, they consented
that a few of us should go with the man, and sent the rest of us
back. I do not know who this man was.

Most, but not all, of the eyewitness accounts took the side
of the citizenry. One man, an exception to the rule, insisted
that the

military did nothing but pass slowly and quietly through the
street. And *how* were these citizen soldiers treated, called out by
the authorities to assist in preserving the peace of the city? Without having used the least violence, or uttered one offensive word,
they were barbarously and brutally assaulted with stones. These
are facts to which hundreds can testify. It was not until every
window in the building almost had been smashed, the lives of
those within endangered, and the civil officers personally attacked
that the military appeared at all; and it was not until the military
themselves, without a shadow of provocation had been assailed,
that the firing commenced. You should recollect the anecdote of
old General Baron Steuben, a warm hearted Veteran of '76. During the heat of the Doctor's Riot in this city, while endeavoring
to deter the Governor from giving orders for the infantry to fire
on the mob, he himself was struck by a missile, stung by the
anguish of the blow, in one moment all his philanthropic arguments were forgotten, and he cried out as he fell, "Fire, Governor, fire, don't wait a moment longer."

By the time the last volley had been fired, the performance inside had finished and Macready had gotten safely out
of the theatre. In spite of all the competition from outside,
"the constant crushing and thumping of stones and the ter-
rible yells of the crowd in the street," Macready had gamely,

if hastily, proceeded through the last scene of the play. During the banquet scene, Mr. Povey approach Macready and urged him to cut out part of the play and bring it to a close. Macready turned upon him "very sharply" and replied, "I have consented to do this thing—to place myself here, and whatever the consequence I must go through with it—it must be done; I can not cut out. The audience has paid for so much, and law compels me to give it; they would have cause for riot, if all were not properly done." At the close of the third act, when Macready went below to change his costume, the military were marching around the building. He must have wondered if he would ever get back on stage to continue. "The battering at the building, doors, and windows growing, like the fiends at the Old Woman of Berkely's burial, louder and louder. Water was running down fast from the ceiling to the floor of my room and making a pool there. I inquired; the stones hurled in had broken some of the pipes."

Macready went back up and raced through the fourth and fifth acts without interruption. By this time a large share of the audience had left their seats and were gathered in the lobby, unable to get out of the building. Macready wrote that "the furious noises against the building and from without waxed louder and more fierce. . . . Whenever a missile did effectual mischief in its discharge it was hailed with shouts outside; stones came in through the windows, and one struck the chandelier; the audience removed for protection behind the walls; the house was considerably thinned, gaps of unoccupied seats appearing in the audience part. The fifth act was heard, and in the very spirit of resistance I flung my whole soul into every word I uttered, acting my very best and exciting the audience to a sympathy even with the glowing words of fiction, whilst these dreadful deeds of

real crime and outrage were roaring at intervals in our ears
and rising to madness all round us." One spectator reported
that there was no need for any artificial means to convey to
the audience that Macbeth's castle was sustaining an assault.
The outside noise surpassed anything that the stage appli-
ances could supply.

"The death of Macbeth," according to Macready, "was
loudly cheered, and on being lifted up and told that I was
called, I went on, and, with action earnestly and most emphatically expressive of my sympathy with them and my
feelings of gratefulness to them, I quitted the New York
stage amid the acclamations of those before me." Through
it all, according to the testimony of his associates, "Macready
bore himself with commanding dignity and firmness." Mr.
Chippendale, the stage manager, insisted that Macready was
the only "truly courageous man" on hand that evening.

Just before the final curtain, a violent attack was made by
the mob on one of the doors, which was partly forced. A
body of policemen, armed with their short clubs, sallied
forth and secured a number of the leaders, who were
brought in and placed in the barroom under the parquet.
These rioters, to the number of thirty or forty, battered
down the partition of the room with their feet and then attempted to crawl out at the bottom by the holes so made. A
sronger guard was assigned, and no one succeeded in making his escape.

At the close of the play the audience was ushered out
through the door nearest Broadway on the Astor Place side
and moved rapidly toward Broadway through a file of infantry with fixed bayonets. The soldiers had just cleared
part of the area in their maneuver around the building, so
the audience was able to pass unmolested. This was just before the first volley of gunfire.

Macready was still in his dressing room when the soldiers first fired.

When washed and half dressed, persons came into my room—consternation on the faces of some; fear, anxiety, and distress on those of others. "The mob were getting stronger; why were not the military sent for." "They were here." "Where, Why did they not act?" "Why did not they disperse the mob then?" These questions and answers, with many others, were passed to and fro among the persons around me whilst I was finishing my hasty toilet, I occasionally putting in a question or remark. Suddenly we heard a volley of musketry: "Hark! what's that?" I asked. "The soldiers have fired." "My God!" I exclaimed. Another volley, and another; The question among those surrounding me (there were, that I remember, Ruggles, Judge Kent, D. Colden, R. Emmett, a friend of his in some official station, Fry, Sefton, Chippendale, and I think the performer who played Malcolm) was, which way was I to go out? News came that several were killed; I was really insensible to the degree of danger in which I stood, and saw at once—there being no avoidance—there was nothing for it but to meet the worst with dignity, and so I stood prepared: They sent some one to reconnoitre, and urged the necessity of a change in my appearance. I was confident that people did not know my person, and repeated this belief. They overbore all objections, and took the drab surtout of the performer of Malcolm, he taking my black one; they insisted too, that I must not wear my hat; I said, "Very well; lend me a cap." Mr. Sefton gave me his, which was cut all up the back to go upon my head.

Thus dressed and with his protective entourage, Macready was let out into Eighth Street, which had been completely cleared by the military and was now held by the police. The party moved rapidly away from the theatre without being recognized and crossed Broadway, but, instead of going down Broadway to the New York Hotel, Robert Emmett insisted that they go to his house, where Macready would be secure from the mob. Emmett's uncle, the Irish patriot, must have turned in his grave to find his nephew's sentiments thus allied.

While Macready was safely settling himself in Emmett's drawing room—"talking of the facts about us, and wondering at myself and my condition, secretly preparing myself for the worst results; viz., falling into the hands of those sanguinary ruffians"—a contingent of the same was on its way to storm the New York Hotel and force Macready out of his lodgings. But this small group, deprived of the moral support of the mob of idle spectators in Astor Place, was driven off by the waiters. Mr. Monnitt, the proprietor, was the only casualty in this engagement. His arm was slightly hurt by a stone thrown by one of the rioters.

By now—Macready having escaped from the theatre, the mob having been pushed back by a third barrage of ball cartridges, and with artillery reinforcements turning into Astor Place from Broadway—General Sandford, for the first time since his arrival on the scene, felt that he had the situation in hand. Before the first volley of gunfire Sandford had made a hasty check of his forces. He had started with three hundred strong. The fifty cavalrymen had been rendered useless by the unruliness of their horses in the first circling of the Opera House, and one hundred men had been posted to protect the Broadway end of the theatre on Astor Place. That left him with just one hundred and fifty men to attack the mob in front of the theatre. Some fifty of these were injured and carried into the Opera House before the first order to fire. With the small remaining force of a hundred men to oppose a mob that has been variously estimated at ten, twelve, fifteen, and even twenty-four thousand, Sandford had sent off to the Arsenal for reinforcements, order-

ing up a detachment of the sixth regiment known as the
Governor's Guard (this was under the command of a Colonel Peers), a company of horse artillery known as Yates's
Battery, and two six-pounder field pieces loaded with grape
and canister. These forces had arrived just after the last volley had been fired. The guns were set up in Astor Place at
either end of the theatre, one facing the Bowery and the
other, Broadway; and the fresh troops were deployed in like
positions, with a small contingent moved into Eighth Street.
With the arrival of the additional military and with their
serious intention to fire having already been all too clearly
demonstrated, the mob began to disperse, carrying off their
dead and wounded.

Inside the Opera House, Sidney Stuart, Clerk of the Police, was commissioned by Judge Edmonds to take the names
and record the number of all the injured police and military.
After the first round, Stuart reported, "There were several
of the military brought in, some half dozen brought in
separately by the police, some of them perfectly senseless;
some policemen were also brought in; also several of the
rioters, mostly young men." He estimated that in the half
hour after the first volley between thirty and forty were
brought in. According to another account, seventy-two police and military were wounded before the first order to fire.
Chief Matsell, struck on the chest with a stone weighing
"twenty pounds and three ounces," reported a week later
that he could still "feel the effects." As the *Morning Courier*
(May 14) pointed out, the "wounds received by the military
were much more severe than most persons supposed from
the fact that they were merely stone cuts and bruises. There
is hardly a more dangerous and disabling wound than the
contusion received from a cobble stone."

Most of the dead and injured were, however, among the

rioters and spectators (chiefly the latter). These casualties
were not brought into the theatre but were treated on the
street, in the various drugstores in the neighborhood, at the
Fifteenth Ward Police Station, and at the City Hospital.
Although most of the casualties were in the neighborhood
of Mrs. Langdon's house and at the Bowery corner of Lafayette Place and Astor Place, the musket balls seem to have
sprayed the entire neighborhood. The public house at 23
East Eighth Street had been hit by three of them, all "three
of which entered the dwelling, one of them through the
drawing-room windows, and into a closet almost hitting
children who were in bed." The "Oyster Theatre," kept by
a colored man at the southeast corner of Lafayette Place
and Astor Place, "was pierced by two bullets, one of them
going through, at the upper part of the frame, and, being
turned down, wounded in the face an old woman in the
house, but did not do her any serious injury." Another ball
pierced the doorpost of Mr. Hill's house at 23 Third Avenue,
and two or three passed through an exhibitions tent in the
next lot. The store at the corner of Third Avenue and St.
Mark's Place was struck several times. These establishments
were some hundred and fifty yards away from the theatre.

The newspaper men ranging over the scene faithfully and
minutely reported the casualties. At the Fifteenth Ward
Police Station there were "seven men killed and one who
still lives, but a ball passed through his head, scattering the
brains about." At Vauxhall Garden, near the corner of the
Bowery and Astor Place, a dead man was stretched out on
a billiard table. Seven men, one boy, and one lady were carried on shutters along Broadway to Dr. Chilton's drugstore
at the corner of Broadway and Eighth Street. A colored
woman who lived in a small cottage opposite the Langdon
house was shot through the cheek while lying in bed. Eight

persons were treated in the drugstore of Messrs. Burtnett and Powell, at the corner of St. Mark's Place and Third Avenue. S. F. Cornell was shot through the neck, "severing the jugular vein," and died in the drugstore at the corner of Fourth Street and Broadway.

The newspaper death notices read like a coroner's or pathologist's report. Thomas Kiernan (previously referred to) was killed by a "ball entering the face under the orbit of the eye and lodging in the brain." Owen Burns, a cartman, was killed by another ball "which penetrated the skull on the right side and lodged in the brain." Others among the dead were: Timothy Burns a printer, age sixteen, "shot in the right breast, the ball perforating both lungs and coming out on the left side of the back"; William Butler, a ship-joiner in the employ of Mr. Strickland, killed by a "ball entering the right cheek and lodging in the base of the brain"; Neil Gray Mellis, nephew to ex-alderman Neil Gray, a liquor merchant of 119 Grand Street, "shot in the left breast, the ball having passed through the heart"; George Lincoln, a sailor from East Cambridge, Massachusetts, "shot in the right side of the abdomen, perforating the intestines"; George W. Brown, a twenty-year-old clerk, received "a ball in the left breast which went out just below the shoulder-blade on the same side having gone through the lungs." Brown, it appears, "was standing peaceably by the iron railing on the opposite side of the street. He resided with his mother at 472 Pearl Street, and was taken home a corpse."

The wounded were also carefully noted by the reporters. James Boulton was "shot in the left eye, the ball lodging behind the ear." Stephen Ellwood received an identical injury and was "insensible in the City Hospital." Frederick Gillespie, a small boy, was shot through the feet and taken home. Stephen Kehoe received a "ball directly under the

eye which lodged in the jaw bone near the ear." Philip Liv-
ingston was standing in St. Mark's Place when he received a
shot "in the forearm which came out near the thumb." His
arm was later amputated. William E. Russell, a Wall Street
lawyer, had his left arm shattered while he was crossing
Lafayette Place on his way to his residence on Fourth
Avenue. Two men were shot while descending from the
Harlem cars on the Bowery, one hundred and fifty yards
from the theatre; James Stewart, a retired merchant of the
firm of Coley, Stewart and Co., of Mobile, was "struck by a
ball in the neck," and Asa Collins, a commercial house agent,
received "a ball entering the neck just below the larynx and
passing down into the right lung."

Whenever possible, the reporters augmented these clinical
accounts with pathetic or even tear-jerking particulars. Timothy McGuire, age nineteen, "the only support of a widowed
mother, was standing immediately in the main entrance to
the theatre. At the first discharge of the musketry he received
a ball which entered the abdomen on the left side, midway
between the pelvis and the ribs, passed through the body
and escaped about two inches on the right of the spine. He
expired a few hours after receiving the wounds." Henry
Otten, a grocer, was shot through the stomach and died in
the Fifteenth Ward Station House. "His aged mother was
present and her lamentations were truly heart rending."

John McKinley, another native of Ireland, was also killed
by a musket ball passing through his abdomen. His cousin,
William Tremble, gave a full account (reported in the
New York *Herald* on May 16) of their fatal visit to the
scene.

We were both standing together in the square at the rear of
the Opera House. I had hold of John's arm and we were looking
on. After the first discharge by the military, we started to go to-

wards the Bowery. After going some distance, some persons gave
a cheer; the deceased turned around to look towards them, and
at that moment he was shot. We started to run; he said to me,
"Billy, I am wounded." He spoke very low; I did hardly believe
him. We turned into Fourth Avenue and ran up as far as Ninth
Street. At this time the deceased became faint; myself and another young man took hold of him and carried him into a porter
house at the corner of Ninth Street and Broadway, kept by Mr.
Jones. A Doctor was sent for to dress the wound. He survived
only until Sunday.

George W. Gedney, a Wall Street broker and a "tall fine
looking man," was shot through the head while standing in
Astor Place. "There are circumstances connected with the
death of this gentleman peculiarly distressing. He was married about two years since, and one of his brothers-in-law was
a member of the National Guards. Another brother-in-law,
not knowing that Mr. Gedney was away from home, went
to the Opera House at a late hour (having heard of the riot)
in search of his brother-in-law who was in the military.
While there he was induced to go to the Sixteenth Ward Station House to see the corpses lying there. The first one he saw
was that of his other brother-in-law. The brother-in-law
attached to the National Guard, on seeing the corpse, was
nearly crazed at the idea that he might have inflicted the
mortal wound." Another account described the young Mrs.
Gedney at home, anxiously awaiting her husband, "the
first night he had been out at night, without her, since their
marriage. She waited until four o'clock in the morning in
an agony of terror, when, unable to endure the suspense any
longer, she rushed into the street, went to the house of one of
her husband's friends, roused him from his slumber, and
begged him to go and seek for her husband. The man went,
and found poor Gedney a cold corpse. Mrs. Gedney was sit-

ting at the window when he returned, and motioned for him
to come to her, but he shook his head mournfully, and passed
by in silence. She knew that her beloved husband was no
more."

As might be expected from such a scattering of musket
balls, there were some hairbreadth escapes. A ball went
through the hat of one man, tearing it to pieces, but not
injuring him. John Byrne, while standing near the door of
the public house at 23 Eighth Street, received a bullet through
his overcoat which tore out under his armpit without doing
him the slightest injury. Mrs. Brennard, the housekeeper
for Mrs. Kernochan, at the corner of Second Avenue and
Ninth Street, "was passing up the Bowery on her way home
leaning on the arm of a gentleman. She was struck by a ball
in her left thigh which passed through the fleshy part of this
and the right thigh without injuring the large vessels or the
bones."

Many of the injured rioters protested their innocence, even
those who were struck on the head while stooping to pick
up stones, and those whose pockets were found to be full
of rocks. Henry Burquist, better known as "Harry Bluff," of
510 Pearl Street, was struck by a ball in the right shoulder
which came out behind the right arm. Dr. Cheeseman, the
doctor in attendance at the Fifteenth Ward Police Station,
found it necessary to operate on Burquist's shoulder. Before
beginning to operate, he held some preliminary conversation
(reported in the *Evening Post* for May 15) with his patient:

"Friend, in what position was thee holding thy arm when thee
received thy wound?"

"I don't know," replied Burquist.

"Was thee cheering, waving thy hand in the air?" asked the
doctor.

"No," answered Burquist.

"Well, then," said the doctor, "thee must have been doing the other thing, (throwing a stone) else thee could not have been wounded in this manner."

With the wounded and dead scattered about in the various establishments in the area, no clear count of the casualties was immediately available. The reporters' guesses ran from ten to fifteen dead and twenty to thirty wounded. Even now, with all the newspaper reports, and the accounts of the Coroner's Inquest available, it is difficult to be certain of the final figures. Are Thomas Brennan and Thomas Bulman the same person; Matthew Carhart, Mathew Cahill, Mathew Cahan, one or three? Were there both a James and a John McDonald, or was it McDonnel? One can only guess, but it is certain that at least twenty-two died that night (the night of May 10), and another nine within the next five days. Forty-eight wounded civilians, in addition to the fifty to seventy police and military, were identified by name. Many more injuries undoubtedly went unreported. It is safe to say that thirty-one were killed and at least a hundred and fifty injured. Most of these casualties were probably innocent of any part in instigating the affair. The real rioters seem to have done a good job of dodging the musket balls, for those rounded up by the police in the course of the evening were still hail and hearty.

Even though forced into a defensive position throughout most of the battle, the police had managed to arrest and drag into the Opera House eighty-six of the rioters. These were housed in the theatre for the night, "their presence [according to the *Courier and Enquirer* for May 11] being considered partial security against the burning of the building." In the morning (May 11) they were transferred to Jefferson Market and brought before Justice Mountfort. Twenty-one were discharged at noon for lack of evidence against them. Of the remainder, three were released under $1,000 bail, two under $500, and twenty-two under $300. The rest were committed to prison awaiting trial.

Among those held without bail were the rioters who had attempted to set fire to the building: William Sparks, Robert Bennett, Robert Miller, James McLean, and Charles Tappen. All of these had police records, and their complicity in the affair must have been known to a good many of those inside the theatre. Even Ned Buntline did not escape arrest, but he did manage to get himself released under $1,000 bail the next day.

The arrested were mostly young men. They ranged in age from fifteen to thirty-one, but well over half of them were under twenty. Unlike many political demonstrations in the twentieth century, the Astor Place riot included no students. The rioters were machinists, butchers, organ builders, hucksters, printers, porters, sailmakers, clerks, marble cutters, plumbers, cork merchants, shoemakers, paper folders, carpenters, and gunsmiths. Only one indicated "no business," and one (Ned Buntline) labeled himself an editor.

By 1:00 A.M. the area around the theatre was comparatively quiet. Little knots of men were standing here and there talking over the affair, but, "with one or two exceptions, in a calm and reasonable manner." After the final volley of gunfire, there had been an attempt to rally the rioters for a meeting in Vauxhall Gardens, but the active forces had become so badly disorganized by that time that nothing came of this move. The police and military were safely in control of the building, and all the approaches were securely manned. The military maintained their stations through the night. Between five and six in the morning, one witness reported, "we saw several of the bruised and wounded National Guardsmen taken from the Opera House in carriages."

The account of Macready's last few hours in New York is based upon his diary. Shortly after the riot, fearful reports were brought in by David Colden and Richard Emmett, who had been reconnoitering the Astor Place neighborhood at regular intervals, so it was decided that the only safe course was for Macready to get out of the city as rapidly as possible. Robert Emmett sent his brother Richard to the livery stable to order a carriage and a good pair of horses to be at Emmett's door at four o'clock in the morning (of May 11) "to take a doctor to some gentleman's house near New Rochelle." When Richard returned, he announced that he had seen an omnibus driving furiously down the street followed by a crowd shouting, "Macready's in the omnibus; they've killed twenty of us, and by G—— we'll kill him." This alarming intelligence must have settled any last-minute doubts that Macready might have had. Nevertheless, according to his account, the night passed uneventfully enough. After all arrangements had been made for leaving early in the morning, Robert "went to bed to his wife," and Macready and Richard "went down into the comfortable office below before a good fire and, by the help of a cigar, to count the slow hours till four o'clock. We talked and he dozed. I listened to the sounds of the night, and thought of home, and what would be the anguish of hearts there if I fell in this brutal outbreak; but I resolved to do what was right and becoming."

The actual departure also proceeded without incident: "The clock struck four; we were on the move; Robert came down; sent Richard to look after the carriage. All was still in the dawn of morning, but we waited some ten minutes— an age of suspense—the carriage arrived. Stepping into the carriage, a covered phaeton, we turned up Fifth Avenue, and were on our way to safety. We met only market carts, butchers' or gardeners', and labourers going to their early work; the morning was clear and fresh, and the air was cooling to my forehead, hot and aching with want of sleep. The scenery through which we passed, crossing the Manhattan, giving views of the various inlets of the sound, diversified with gentlemen's seats, at any other time would have excited an interest in me, now one's thought or series of thoughts, with wanderings to home and my beloved ones, gave me no time for passing objects. I thought as we passed Harlem Station, it would never have done to have ventured here." After a hasty breakfast in New Rochelle, Macready was safely on the early morning train for Boston.

What of Forrest on this tragic evening? With New York theatrical activity centered for the night inside and immediately outside the triangle bounded by Astor Place, Eighth Street, and Broadway, and with the ten or twenty thousand gathered on that site, the other theatres might have been expected to close down; but they did not. Forrest was on in *The Gladiator* and was wildly cheered by a large crowd. He appeared before the curtain to acknowledge the applause but made no speech. At the Bowery Hamblin's *Macbeth* had attracted a "large and brilliant audience"; Burton's Theatre, with *Romance and Reality,* and the National, with *The Enchanter,* also had plenty of paying customers; and the minstrel companies, the "microcosmic views," and the exhibits at Barnum's Museum were all well attended. Macready and Forrest had stirred up enough business for everyone.

Rally at City Hall Park

Riots and talk of riots had been in the air. At the end of April the newspapers had been filled with accounts of the mob assaults on the Government buildings in Canada. On April 25 a rebellious contingent of the Orange party appeared before the Parliament buildings in Montreal to protest the acts of the Assembly. Before the rioters were brought under control, they had broken most of the windows with stones and had set fire to one of the wings. Destroyed in the blaze was one of the most valuable libraries in North America, including all legislative journals and records accumulated since 1791.

During the early part of May there had been a series of

riots on the Hudson River Railroad resulting from the strikes
for higher wages. Many of those who were willing to work
had been assaulted, and several had been killed.

On Friday morning, May 11, in the cold light of the post-
mortems, it was clear that neither side had won a decisive
victory at Astor Place. To be sure, the forces of law and order
had held the Opera House, and Macready had escaped without injury. But the rowdies had succeeded in disrupting the
performance, the officials had been obliged to call out the
military, the killed and injured were mostly innocent bystanders, and Macready had been forced out of the city. Even
with a large number of the rioters locked up, the sights and
sounds around the city on Friday did not suggest that the
episode was finished.

The shipyards and other places of business were deserted.
It was a cool but pleasant morning, and instead of going to
their work men gathered in bars and on street corners to
discuss the events of the past night. Rumors—some of which
had been published—were apprehensively passed from group
to group. "A riotous organization of the most formidable
character was in progress." "Two hundred 'killers' were
arriving from Philadelphia." "A scene still more bloody than
that of the preceding night was to be anticipated." "Fire-arms
had been purchased in large quantities by persons riotously
disposed." "The friends of law and order were urged to
register their names at one of the eighteen police stations to
be commissioned as special constables."

The degree of continuing interest in the riot is indicated
by the *Herald's* statement (May 12) "that no fewer than
thirty-three thousand five hundred copies of the paper, con-
taining our full and graphic account of the whole melancholy affair, were disposed of, and circulated all over the
city." The Empire Club, symbol of anti-aristocratic senti-

ments, was shrouded in crepe in memory of the persons killed in the riot. The bodies of those who had lost their lives were gruesomely laid out in various establishments in the Opera House neighborhood. One Washington newspaper man reported, "In coming down town from the Opera House through the Bowery, I saw three of the dead bodies of the rioters in a police station-house, and thousands of people were passing the room in hurried succession to look upon them—a sad sight, and calculated to increase the excitement of the rioters. Six or eight dead bodies, I was told, were also exhibited in Mercer Street."

During the morning several ladies made their appearance at the scene of the action and inquired for friends thought to be among the victims. According to the *Herald* (May 12), "One aged woman, with tears streaming down her pallid face, sought her son; but he was among the fallen. His body had been conveyed to the Seventeenth Ward Station House, where were congregated about a thousand persons, in the greatest possible state of excitement. The aged mother forced her way through the crowd, and discovering the lifeless body of her son, fell upon him and wept in agony. He had not been a participator in the fearful work, but stood a spectator when the fatal bullet deprived him of life. The large crowd gathered there swore to avenge his death, even at the cost of their own lives."

Even with eighty-six of the rioters under arrest, there were enough of them at large to organize a public protest meeting to be held in City Hall Park at six o'clock on Friday evening. Early in the day placards announcing this meeting were posted in conspicuous places throughout the city. Some read quite simply:

To the Park!

Citizens of New York opposed to the destruction of human life are requested to assemble in the Park at 6 o'clock this evening, Friday, May 11, to express public opinion upon the lamentable occurrence of last night!!

Others were openly inflammatory:

AMERICANS!
Arouse! The Great Crisis
Has Come!!
Decide now whether English
ARISTOCRATS!!
and
FOREIGN RULE!
Shall triumph in this
AMERICA'S METROPOLIS,
or whether her own
SONS
whose fathers once compelled the base-born miscreants to succumb, shall meanly lick the hand that strikes, and allow themselves to be deprived of the liberty of opinion—so dear to every true American heart.
AMERICANS!!
Come out! and dare to own yourselves sons of the true hearts of '76!
America.

All during the day there was a large crowd gathered in the park in front of City Hall and the Empire Club. In the afternoon a group of volunteer workers erected a stand for the public speakers.

The area of the Opera House was also thickly populated throughout the entire day. A newspaper account reported the presence of "fashionable parties, both in carriages and on foot," who crowded together with the commoners to get a look at the scene of battle. And it was easy to imagine the

ferocity of the action from the evidence at hand. All the
window panes in the Opera House had been completely shattered in spite of the protective boards. One of the Astor Place
doors was completely smashed, and one on Eighth Street was
badly damaged. The entire area was strewn with bricks and
stones. Mrs. Langdon's house had suffered almost as much
damage. There were twenty conspicuous bullet marks on
the wall, "some of them of very large size." One window
was broken in, and the heavy iron railing around the north
side of the residence had been wrenched from its fastenings
in the wall. Evidently these iron spikes had been used as
weapons. Many of the bricks had been dislodged from the
wall. "Most of these indentations, exhibiting the red brick
in contrast with the dark coat of paint with which the wall
was covered, were so high that they were manifestly the
result of the first volley fired over the heads of the people."

The windows of Dr. Chilton's drugstore, at the corner of
Ninth Street and Broadway, were broken. A bullet had
gone through the door casing of the house on the corner of
Eighth Street and the Bowery, and another through one of
the second-story windows. Large splotches of blood remained on the sidewalks, indicating the direction taken by
the wounded or by those who were carrying them.

One of the "fashionable parties" who visited the scene on
Friday morning was Philip Hone, who lived at 714 Broadway, a short distance south of the Opera House. Hone, of
course, reflected the views of his class. He marked Forrest
as a "vulgar, arrogant loafer, with a pack of kindred rowdies
at his heels." Macready he found a thoroughgoing "gentleman." On the eleventh, Hone made the following entry in
his diary: "I walked up this morning to the field of battle
in Astor Place. The Opera House presents a shocking spectacle and the adjacent buildings were smashed with bullet

holes. Mrs. Langdon's house looked as if it had withstood a siege. Groups of people were standing around, some justifying the interference of the military, but a large proportion were savage as tigers with the smell of blood."

Workmen were again boarding up the windows of the Opera House, and again a city cart was hauling away all the loose paving stones. With the withdrawal of the military at daybreak, a large detachment of police had taken over the defensive duties, but they were kept out of sight within the theatre, "the doors and windows of which seemed hermetically sealed." Remembering the night before, the "stars" felt little security in being cooped up inside the building. One of the officers, when asked if he expected any further disturbance, replied authoritatively, "Yes, we apprehend the hardest night to-night that has ever been known in the United States."

Late in the forenoon Macready's acting company gathered on stage to rehearse *Richelieu,* but they were quickly dismissed, and a notice was posted on the doors of the theatre announcing that the "house was being closed by order of the lessees." This information was also carried in the newspaper ads: "In consequence of the injuries sustained by this establishment during the riot in the streets last evening it will be unavoidably closed until the necessary repairs can be made." The notice reappeared in the press every day for the next week.

All the journals were, of course, filled with the riot. Each had its own full and detailed story of the events and each its own interpretation. Most agreed that law and order had to be maintained. The *Tribune:* "Animosity, passion, excitement must yield to the necessity of preserving the Public Peace and the Supremacy of the Law!" The *Post:* "It is impossible for us today to discuss the propriety of the proceedings which have resulted so disastrously, which have hurried so many of our fellow-citizens into eternity and plunged so many into the deepest affliction. But we have a firm conviction that the municipal authorities acted from the best of motives, with a desire to prevent and to avoid bloodshed, and that they employed the means which they supposed best adapted to that end." The *Globe*: "The sanctity of Freedom's shrine in New York City has been desecrated, but her own honor is untarnished."

Not all agreed, however, on the wisdom of the Mayor's handling of the affair. The *Herald* felt that the theatre should have been closed, or, at any rate, that the Mayor should have issued a proclamation warning citizens against "participating even in the most passive manner." The *True Sun* insisted that he had "committed a most unfortunate blunder, to call it by its mildest name, in calling out the troops." The *Tribune* could not "help thinking the intervention of the military with ball cartridges, uncalled for." The *Courier and Enquirer,* on the other hand, held that if the Mayor "had ordered the theatre to be closed, he would simply have *sided with the mob.* He would have elevated their edicts into laws! He would have declared distinctly, that the laws of the city, and the personal right of every one of its inhabitants, must bow to the will of an infuriated mob. If Macready had not appeared, the whole world would have been justified in saying, that the laws of New York could not protect a man in the exercise of his lawful calling, that they were powerless, in the presence of an organized mob."

The unhappy alignment of forces in the controversy—aristocrats on one side, rowdies on the other—was hinted at in the papers but was not at this time explored in any detail. This was a touchy subject for the press. The *Herald* recognized that the riot had introduced a "new aspect in the minds of many, nothing short of a controversy and collison between those who have been styled the 'exclusive,' or 'upper-ten,' and the great popular masses." The *Courier and Enquirer,* although hoping that order was now permanently restored, could see "that the elements of mischief are still at work. The passions of the worst portion of our people have been aroused. They are skillfully fomented by adroit and unprincipled men, who seek to make personal or political capital from them."

The Philadelphia *Public Ledger,* in an editorial dated May 11, placed the blame for the whole affair on the New York newspapers. "Very little perspicacity is necessary to discover that, in all these disgraceful proceedings, the mob, the rioters, the persons who throw the eggs, are the least at fault. This is their vocation; the things on which they are versed; it is their mother's milk. Few of them know better, none of them are encouraged to do better, and when they do it, nobody is surprised. 'It's just like them.' The guilty are the mischief makers who blow up a controversy in the newspapers, and the busy bodies who spread the excitement by talking, and then going to see the fun. It is needless for us to say that the law ought to visit such disturbers of the peace (the editors), such traitors to a profession whose every duty is the maintenance of law through moral force, with its good wholesome penalties of fine and imprisonment."

These and similar sentiments were widely echoed around the city, but primary attention was centered on the immediate prospects for the day at hand. What was the Mayor going to do? What action would the military take? Would the meeting in the Park precipitate another riot?

During the day a number of official gatherings took place. In the morning the Mayor went into conference with a "group of our most estimable citizens." William Kent,

Samuel B. Ruggles, Judge Duer, Judge Edmonds, General Sandford, and Recorder Tallmadge were present, and all agreed that some positive action had to be taken. Also, on the morning of the same day the Grand Jury of the Court of Sessions met and prepared a document to be promulgated in the name of the Court. "The Grand Inquest, taking into consideration the highly excited state of the public feeling, growing out of the riot of the last twenty-four hours would present the necessity of adopting such conciliatory measures as may tend to quell the excitement and recommend that the performances at the Opera House be suspended for the present." This suggestion was accepted by the lessees of the theatre without any opposition. The Jury also informed the Court that they would "cheerfully cooperate in any measures thought necessary for the preservation of the peace of the city." The Recorder thanked those who had participated in the Inquest for their aid and told them that he would lay their communication before the Mayor.

Dr. Walters, "our very efficient Coroner," after a hasty survey of the fatalities, issued a notice which was posted about the city just before noon.

> CORONER'S OFFICE, *May 11, 1849*
>
> Persons who witnessed the wounding or death of individuals during the riot at the Opera House Theatre, in Astor Place, on Thursday evening last, will please to meet at the Coroner's Office, Halls of Justice, Centre Street, on Saturday, May 12th, at 11 o'clock, A.M.
>
> WM. A. WALTERS, *Coroner.*

He also served subpoenas on all the public officials who had had any connection with the riot.

At two o'clock in the afternoon the Mayor issued a proclamation:

The Mayor of the City, while deeply deploring the loss of life which has resulted from the maintenance of the law during the past night, reminds all the citizens that the peace of the City must be maintained.

He calls on all good citizens to sustain the Magistracy. The efforts of the authorities will be considerate, will be humane, but they ought and must be firm.

He recommends all citizens, for some days, to remain as much as possible within their own dwellings, and abstain from swelling public assemblages, and from all acts that tend to encourage the riotously disposed.

The effect of crowds is to expose the innocent to the injury arising from the measures which must be taken.

THE PEACE OF THE CITY MUST AND SHALL BE MAINTAINED, by the whole civil and military power of the County.

It should always be remembered that the military is but a portion of the Police of our City, composed of our own fellow-citizens, who are under special obligation to maintain the supremacy of their own laws.

C. S. WOODHULL, Mayor

MAYOR'S OFFICE, May 11.

The Mayor soon discovered, however, that the situation demanded more than proclamations. Just after his notice had been posted, he was informed that a Mr. James McCullough who ran a gun store on the corner of Front Street and Maiden Lane, "had been applied to by some parties who wished to borrow *two thousand muskets* for two or three days, offering to pay well for the use of them, and to give security for their return." Captain Wiley, of the First Ward, was dispatched to Mr. McCullough's with orders to remove the muskets to the Arsenal. At three o'clock the Mayor called a special and secret session of his Board of Aldermen to determine what precautionary measures should be taken that evening. All agreed that the military must be brought out in force and that this must be done before the meeting in City Hall Park had a chance to fan up another riot.

General Sandford was ordered to muster his forces at the Washington Parade Ground (Washington Square) at four o'clock. Sandford called on the Fourth Infantry Brigade under Brigadier General Ewen to supply the bulk of the men. On hand from this Brigade were the Tenth Regiment under the command of Colonel Halsey, the Eleventh under Colonel Morris, and the Twelfth under Colonel Stebbins. In addition, there were four troops of horse artillery under the command of Colonel Ryer, and one squadron of cavalry, both of these from the First Brigade. Colonel Warner's Fifth Regiment from the Second Brigade also appeared for action, along with a small detachment from the Veteran's Artillery Corps. A request was sent to Commodore McKeever at the Navy Yard for a contingent of marines, but they never appeared. Another requisition was sent by the Governor to the Commanding Officer of Fort Columbus to hold a body of regulars in readiness should they be needed in preserving the peace.

By six o'clock on Friday evening there were some two thousand men going through their drills and receiving their rounds of ball cartridges, "all looking very well, and ready at a moment's notice to do the bidding of their commanders." At six-thirty they formed in marching order and defiled into Eighth Street, moving toward the Opera House to join forces with the nine hundred policemen and one thousand special constables who had been sworn in that day and were now on duty. When the military left the parade ground, there were only some two or three hundred spectators on hand to watch their maneuvers. Everyone else seems to have been at the meeting in City Hall Park.

At six o'clock, in this area, there was a crowd that has been variously estimated at five, fifteen, and even twenty-five thousand. The meeting got off to a bad start. When W. W. Mansterstook rose to make the opening remarks, "A sudden crash and noise was heard; the high platform, which was loaded with people, suddenly gave way and fell to pieces." The entire platform group was sent sprawling on the ground. Although no one on the platform was injured, a small boy standing nearby was crushed to death beneath the falling timbers. But even this calamity necessitated only a temporary interruption; the boy was carried off to Rushton's Drug Store, and the meeting proceeded. Mansterstook climbed on a table that had survived the destruction, engineered the appointment of George A. Halsey and Albert H. Waggoner as secretaries, made a brief statement of the purpose of the gathering, and then introduced the first speaker. This was a Mr. Strahan, known to the local press as the "Tammany Hall Spouter." His speech and the immediately following speeches of Captain Rynders and Mike Walsh were all recorded in the *Herald* for May 12.

Fellow citizens, in view of the deep disgrace that has fallen on our city, in consequence of the conduct of some of our city rulers, last evening, the following resolutions are submitted for your consideration:—

Resolved, That we love the peace, are law abiding citizens, and devoted to the welfare of this, the first city of the Union, but, above all, we cannot sanction the murder of innocent men by them whose sworn duty is to protect them in all the rights of American citizens.

Resolved, That we believe it to be the duty of our city authorities, if a riot takes place, or if they have good reason to believe that a riot, involving the destruction of life or property, will take place, to exhaust the civil power of the county before resorting to the military, which is, in fact, the right arm of despotism, and ought to be the last resort of Americans. And here we must condemn the Mayor of our city, for not causing the Astor Place Opera House to be closed, when he knew (as he says) that a riot would ensue if it were opened.

Resolved, That we look upon the sacrifice of human lives in the vicinity of the Astor Place Opera House, last night, as the most wanton, unprovoked, and murderous outrage ever perpetrated in the civilized world; and that the aiders, abettors, and instigators of that unparalleled crime, deserve, and shall receive the lasting censure and condemnation of this community.

Resolved, That in our opinion, it is the imperative duty of the Grand Jury of this county to indict the Mayor, Recorder, and the Sheriff of this city, for ordering the military to fire on the citizens, during the disastrous and bloody tragedy of last night.

Resolved, That we mingle our tears and lamentations with the mourning friends and relatives of the men, women, and children, who have fallen victims to the pride, tyranny, and inhumanity of those who, "dressed in a brief authority," have shown a higher regard for the applause of those who courted a fatal issue than for the lives of their fellow citizens.

.   .   .   .

Resolved, That a committee be appointed by the Chairman, to take testimony in relation to the lamentable affair of last night, for the purpose of presenting it to the proper authorities and our fellow-citizens.

Resolved, That we owe it to ourselves, to the high character of our city, to the genius of our institutions, to the vindication of a large body of our fellow-citizens from the opprobrious and unfounded charges made against them, to prove to our and their revilers that we respect the rights of others, are neither destructives nor law breakers, and, therefore, will not counsel or countenance the destruction of life or property.

Resolved, That while we are opposed to all violence, in theatres, or elsewhere, we still insist that our citizens have a perfect and indisputable right to express their approbation or disapprobation in all places of public amusement; and we regard the arrest and imprisonment of persons last night, for merely expressing their opinion in the Opera House as only surpassed in atrocity by the outrage perpetrated outside amongst the people.

According to one reporter, "the reading of these ably drawn up and powerful resolutions produced a great and decided impression upon the immense mass, which listened to the reading of them in profound silence. At some of the most striking expressions, such as 'murder of innocent people,' 'indiscreet Mayor,' etc., there was a loud, spontaneous burst of warm and indignant feeling."

In concluding his remarks, Strahan advised the people to go home, "and calmly review and consider what they heard, and, in the course of time, act according to the dictates of a sound and temperate judgment."

Captain Rynders, of the famous Empire Club, then mounted the table and addressed the assembly: "Fellow Citizens, it strikes me that the first thing now in order is to put the resolutions to a vote." This the Chairman did, and the resolutions were "adopted by acclamation." Captain Rynders proceeded as follows:

Fellow Citizens:—When I look upon this vast concourse of citizens assembled here, I am overwhelmed by my feelings at reflecting upon the dreadful calamity which has befallen our city. (Shouts of "Murder, murder.") Yes, fellow citizens, you may well call it murder. I do not say that it has been perpetrated from the mere motive and intention of killing men; I do not say that when they first ordered out the troops they had the intention of murder, but when they gave the word and said "fire," then it was a murderous act, and murder was committed upon inoffensive citizens by the chief magistrate of the proud city of New York— a city where such a thing as a riot has scarcely ever been known

before. Fellow citizens, for what—for whom was this murder
committed? (I hope you will keep order, I hope you will prove
by your conduct this evening, that the working men of our city
are as orderly as the aristocracy.) Why was this murder perpetrated? Was it done for the sake of justice and for the object of
preserving order? (Loud cries of "No, no.") I think not. For
what, then, was it done? To please the aristocracy of the city at
the expense of the lives of inoffending citizens—to please an
aristocratic Englishman, backed by a few sympathetic Americans. It was more important to these aristocrats that Mr. Macready, an Irish-Englishman, should play before them, and that
they should be amused by him for a short hour, than that they
should prevent a riot. . . . Well Macready did play, in dumb show,
and the "stars" were there to see him, and protect him—I mean
our police, who have so distinguished themselves on this occasion.
Now I want to say something in relation to the agency which I
am reported to have had in this matter. . . . I was not hostile to
Mr. Macready because he was an Englishman, but because he
was full of his country's prejudices, from the top of his head to
his feet, if he has any. On this account, I was ready to take a
number of tickets, and manifest my dissatisfaction of his conduct.
It has been said that money was paid to me in order to put him
down. Fellow citizens, it is a base lie. (Loud cheers.) I paid my
own money for the tickets, and a few others paid for other tickets
to be given away. If I did wrong, that was all I did, and I do not
shrink from the responsibility of it. Now, fellow-citizens, as re-
gards the Mayor, I do not wish to speak unkindly of him; I will
merely state the truth; but even the truth in regard to him is too
hard to dwell upon. . . . Yesterday I waited upon the Mayor; Mr.
Matsell, Mr. Wiley, and others can vouch for the truth of what
I say. I told him there was danger of a fearful riot; I said to him,
"For God's sake, stop the proceedings; you are bound to protect
the lives of the citizens." I gave him my advice, and I believe the
Mayor is a man of truth, and he will not deny it. A consultation
was held last night again; I spoke to Alderman Kelly, of the 2d
ward, and asked him if he would not go to the Mayor, and pre-

vail upon him to put a stop to the proceedings. No, it was all in vain; they were determined to be gratified by having Mr. Macready to play for them at the expense of the lives of their fellow citizens. (Three groans were called for, and given by the immense mass with profound solemnity.)

And now, fellow-citizens, I have some remarks to make in relation to the military. They were the slaves of her Majesty of England. They obeyed orders, and gallantly fired, and killed two old ladies and thirty or forty citizens. That same evening, one of our public functionaries boasted, while he was regaling himself in a tavern with his usual beverage, of the murders which had been committed. (Cries of "Three groans for Recorder Tallmadge," to whom it was understood that reference was made.) So I have heard, fellow-citizens, I do not affirm it to be so; but I have heard that it was so. A number of our fellow-citizens, who yesterday at this time were alive and hearty, as we are here, were murdered last night, and are now stark and stiff in death. (Loud groans.) Our National Guards did this, with General Sandford at their head. They have not particularly distinguished themselves upon the field of Mexico—they never drew a sword or shouldered a musket to fight for their country; but last night they shot down a couple of elderly ladies, and a number of peaceable inoffensive citizens. General Sandford would make a field marshal before whom the glory of Ney would be eclipsed. But, if he was to be made one of Napoleon's marshals, it would not be because he could fight, but because of the murders he could boast of having committed. . . . As to the civil force of New York, I do not wish to be so severe upon the Star Police as the gentleman who has preceded me, though, as a class, altogether, they deserve what he has said of them. But I should like to know, if the object of their being called out was to preserve the peace, why were they not in the street instead of being shut up in the theatre? It is the first time one ever heard of police being shut up in a house in order to quell a riot in a street and put a mob down. There they were, drawn up inside the house, in order to revenge the aristocrats of this city against the working classes. . . . Another thing I will mention; it has been said that Mr. Forrest—Edwin Forrest (loud cheering, three cheers for Mr. Forrest)—it has been said that he gave money to pay for putting Macready down. Fellow citizens, it is a lie. (Cries of "It is a lie.") I would give two hundred and fifty dollars to any one who would prove, by good witnesses, that I ever received one cent from Mr. Forrest, or any one, for such a purpose. . . . But, on the other hand, Mr. Macready sent one hundred and twelve tickets to the b'hoys to support him; but one of them, Billy Sparks, said, "I will take your ticket, but I will hiss you." He did so, and he is now in prison for it. (Cries of "Shame! shame!") Mr. Macready is the man who has paid money.

Now, when this meeting breaks up, I hope you will go home like peaceable citizens, and not tear down any houses. Mr. Macready, as you all know, left the city last night, though the men who claim to be exclusives pretended they would sustain him; yet the little man had to run for his life in spite of their promises. (Shouts, "He went upon the telegraph wires.") His baggage followed him this evening. There were some who were for plunging it into the river; but no—God forbid such things should be done. It is not necessary we should have a burning city, though last night I should have been glad to have hung up a dozen of them like rats; but we have had time to reflect, and the feelings of American citizens have had time to recover their ascendancy—feelings always in favor of justice, order, and humanity. Now then, I hope you will disperse quietly and go home peaceably to your habitations, in proper time.

When Rynders finished, loud cries were raised for Mike Walsh. After some delay, Mr. Walsh came forward, ascended the table, and began speaking:

Friends and Fellow-citizens—This is the first time in the history of this city that we have been called upon to deplore a cowardly, base, and murderous attack upon the citizens. So long as the dispute between Forrest and Macready was passive, I took no part in the matter. I did not think it becoming the dignity of an American citizen to make a dispute between two play-actors a national question. But now it has ceased to be a personal matter, and has resolved itself into a war on the part of the public authorities of this city against the lives of the people whom they ought to protect. Not in the whole history of the civilized world has there ever been committed an atrocity equal to that which was perpetrated last night. Even the Czar of Russia, who holds the lives of the people in little better estimation than that of dogs, has always required three rounds of blank cartridges to be fired by the troops before they fire with ball upon the people. . . . The very fact of the commission of this outrage proves that we are the most forbearing people upon the earth. If such a thing had occurred in Paris, the streets would have been soon filled with barricades, raised against the cut-throats, with the Mayor at their head. It is easy to preach peace when we do not mean it, but law and order become a curse when they bring death and desolation into families, and cause the tears of mourning relatives to be shed, calling loud for vengeance. I, myself, was not near the Astor Place theatre last night, but I say that F. A. Tallmadge, Mr. Westervelt, and Mr. Matsell, deserve hanging a thousand times. (Cries of "hang them up—hang them up.") We have had a proclamation from a man, who, by a mere accident of circumstances, has arrived to be Mayor, and, no doubt, there are thousands like him who are drinking the blood of the operatives, who long for the power of an army by which they may oppress and trample the poor man under foot. Where were these National Guards during the late war with Mexico? Where were those gingerbread soldiers? They were drinking punch at their firesides, while it was the poor man who fought the battles of the country. . . . When the Opera House was opened, it was restricted to those only who wore white kid gloves, such was the spirit of pride and presumption of the nabobs of the Fifteenth Ward, who, led by the Mayor, have brought troops to fire upon the people. Who will take care of the families they have made desolate? Will Macready, will Forrest, will Woodhull? No! Let us be dignified, but let us speak strongly and firmly. I say, so help me God, if another shot is fired by these scoundrels, I will, with musket and bayonet in my hand—(The conclusion was lost owing to the applause.)

After Walsh's tirade, the tumult became so great and the excitement so intense that the meeting was adjourned. As the crowd dispersed, there were loud cries of "Vengeance! Vengeance!" and "To the Opera House!" Several thousand moved uptown in the direction of Astor Place.

One reporter, following along in the same direction, stopped off to look in at Forrest's performance at the Broadway. "Forrest was playing with his usual power, in the midst of the tragedy of *Lear*; but the house was very thin." Another report said there were scarcely fifty persons in the house. Forrest had wanted to close the theatre on that night, but the management insisted that such an action "might provoke a feeling unfavorable to the result which was aimed at." There was certainly no inclination on Forrest's part to participate actively in the affair at Astor Place, nor was he urged to do so.

When the crowd arrived at the Opera House, at about half past eight in the evening, the military and the police were in full command of the entire neighborhood. A police cordon extended across Broadway at Eighth Street, and another had been stationed at Waverly Place, "facing outside." Within this line, some ten or twelve feet distant, was another line, two deep, of soldiers. Similar lines were drawn across the Bowery, both above and below Astor Place. Two other police contingents were posted on Broadway, one at Ninth Street and another at Bleecker, to prevent omnibuses and other vehicles from passing through that part of Broadway. A company of mounted troops, riding abreast, galloped up and down the streets all the way around the triangle in which the Opera House was situated, keeping the immediate area completely clear of all intruders. Twelve-pound howitzers, loaded with grape and canister, had been placed on Broadway at Eighth Street and at Waverly Place; another howitzer faced the theatre entrance, and there were two others at the eastern end of the building facing toward the Bowery. The forces were so disposed that only the police were in direct contact with the crowd. But the military backing up the police were out in such numbers that they impressed one observer as being "impregnable save by regular military attack from a force of equal numbers and possessed of greater bravery."

The Opera House itself was occupied by the police. All the entrances but one were closed; the "vaults" were arranged for the reception of prisoners, the dressing-rooms fitted up as surgical hospitals, and the boxes, parquet, and stage thrown open as a general camping ground for the relieved companies. Everything of value had been removed from the interior of the house. Dr. Sayre, General Sandford's regimental surgeon, was in charge of the improvised hospital; he was assisted by Doctors Fisher, Gardiner, Makay, and Smith.

The crowd from the Park meeting, now estimated at some six to seven thousand, had come up Broadway, but, being unable to penetrate beyond Waverly Place, had turned east to the Bowery. From here they began jeering and hooting. They were too far from the troops to make an effective attack with stones even if they had found adequate ammunition. The supply of paving stones had, of course, been largely depleted by the rioters the night before, and the stones that were left had been almost entirely removed that morning by street cleaners. A few shots, thrown from handkerchief slings, were aimed at the dragoons, but only one man was unhorsed.

At the Broadway end of the Opera House everything was comparatively quiet until a soldier on Broadway accidentally dropped his musket, which went off. "The effect was remarkable. He was in the second line which was standing at ease. Instantly every officer and man sprung to his post and the mob fled down Broadway and Waverly Place with the greatest precipitation."

By 9:30 it was evident to the leaders of the mob that a frontal assault would be futile. A few guerrilla-like maneuvers to harrass the military seemed the best course of action. One group skirted around the troops and made its way into the yard of a marble-finishing plant at the corner of the Bowery and Astor Place. This was a good position from which to start an attack, and there was, of course, a ready-made supply of ammunition. Another group erected a barricade, using a wagon and some boxes, at Ninth Street and Fourth Avenue. Some others gained the flat tops of the houses at the corner of the Bowery and Eighth Street. From these positions they launched the only successful barrage of the evening. Two dragoons, O'Halloran and Coyle, were knocked from their horses and were carried into the Opera House; one had been struck in the left eye and the other in the abdomen. Two policemen were also injured and carried in, to be attended by Dr. Sayre and his staff.

But this skirmishing was soon ended. The barricade was carried by detachments of the Thirteenth and Sixteenth Divisions of the police; and the Seventeenth Division cleared the marble-finishing yard and the rooftops. During this assault Recorder Tallmadge and Colonel Wetmore came forward to announce that the mob would be fired on by the soldiers if any more stones were thrown. The rowdies then gave up their attack, retreating farther up the Bowery and attempting to solace themselves by building a large bonfire. They may have wanted warmth, the temperature being barely fifty, or they may have hoped to raise a fire alarm and thus add to the general confusion; but in either case they made themselves more conspicuous to the police, who now advanced and freely rounded up the most obvious offenders. Some sixty were arrested and safely deposited inside the Opera House. These, unlike most of the others who had been arrested on the previous night, were grown men, not boys.

Even had the rioters been goaded on by initial success, as they were the night before, they would have had little chance against the well organized forces of the police and the military. As the man from the *Tribune* (May 12) reported, "We venture to say that no violent mob of such an extent was ever more promptly and successfully quelled. As the Captain of each Division called, the men answered immediately, formed in order, and made a running charge upon the offenders, which was in all cases irresistible. Chief Matsell, as well as the Sheriff, Recorder, and Justices of the Wards, exercised the most constant vigilance so long as there was any apparent danger. When we left at midnight, order was almost entirely restored. Several companies had been discharged for the night, as the streets were quiet, and no sign of disturbance had occurred in any other part of the city."

One minor accident was reported in the ranks of the military. At 1:30 A.M. James P. Wright, a member of the Union Rifle Corps stationed inside the Opera House, had his hand "badly shattered by the explosion of his powder flask, occasioned by indiscreet conduct on the part of one of his comrades."

There had been some fear that an attack might be made

on the Mayor's house and on the residences of other officials,
or even on the homes of those who had signed the letter petitioning Macready to make his scheduled appearance. The
anxiety felt by the Macready supporters is indicated in
George Templeton Strong's diary entry for May 11. "The
houses of the gentlemen who signed the invitation to Macready to perform last night threatened. Judge William Kent
and Mr. Ruggles and some six or seven others of them live
on Union Square and that will, therefore, very probably be
a scene of disturbance. I'm going up now to clean my pistols,
and if possible to get my poor wife's portrait out of harm's
way. Mr. Ruggles is making every arrangement and is a
good deal alarmed." In his entry for the following day, however, Strong suggests that adequate precautions were being
taken by the police and the military. "Yesterday afternoon
was a very hurrying time, running about between my house
and No. 24 to make arrangements for the night. Mrs. Ruggles was brought up to our front parlor, where an extempore
bed was rigged for her. She hadn't left her room for two or
three months before. Poor Ellen's portrait and some other
precious things were sent up. Spent the night till about one
partly with Mr. Ruggles and Judge Kent and partly in reconnoitering the view of operations at Eighth Street and Astor
Place. Everything looked much in earnest there—guns
loaded and matches lighted—everything ready to sweep the
streets with grape at a minute's notice, and the police and
troops very well disposed to do it whenever they should be
told. The mob were in a bitter bad humor but a good deal
frightened, and the only overt acts that were committed on
the Bowery side, were met by prompt measure and with
instant success. Some of the cavalry were badly hit with paving stones, but as soon as the Unwashed were informed that

unless they forthwith took themselves off they'd be treated with a little artillery practice, they scampered."

It is not unlikely that if the rioters had properly assessed the situation and known about the fear that was felt in the Macready camp, they would have pinpointed their attacks on the homes of the various individual petitioners. Fortunately, this strategem was not attempted; though gathered in force at the Opera House, the mob could do little more than watch the maneuvers. By two o'clock on Saturday morning the streets in the area were completely deserted except by the military, who were now standing at ease, all wishing for daylight, when they would be dismissed.

The Coroner's Inquest

CHAPTER TEN

On Saturday morning (May 12), when the military retired from the scene of the riot, only a token force of policemen were on duty. The crowd had completely dispersed, and during the day there was little action around the Opera House. A few women and children promenaded by to view the effects of the riot, but the general excitement seemed to be rapidly subsiding. The Empire Club in Park Row was still covered with the American flag intertwined with black crepe; and in the park in front there were groups of suspicious-looking persons engaged in conversation, but even here, according to the *Courier and Enquirer* (May 14), the "lawless heat of passion had cooled down," and there was no evidence of any further attempt at retaliation. Some small excitement was kicked up by the rumor that a large number of desperadoes from Philadelphia were coming in on the afternoon train to "fraternize with the local rowdies." These "killers" were purportedly led by a famous scoundrel known as the "Panther." They evidently never arrived.

There was another rumor that a meeting was to be called at the Broadway Tabernacle by the friends of law and order "to ratify the conduct of the military." Happily this was called off. Any meeting of Macready sympathizers would assuredly have brought on more violence.

Evidently the proprietor of the New York Hotel believed that there might be another attack on his establishment. He requested the *Express* "to inform the public that Mr. Macready was no longer a resident of the New York Hotel."

There were other brief paragraphs about Macready in the news. He had arrived safely in Boston on Friday evening on the New Haven train and was staying at the home of Mr. Curtis in Chauncey Place. The rumor that "he would be induced to play before our citizens was scotched by the Boston *Journal* (May 12): "Macready will not play in Boston. He is to leave for England Tuesday, the 22d, by the Cunard steamer, Hibernia, and with the avowed determination never to return."

On Friday the evening meeting at City Hall Park had held the center of interest; on the day after all attention was focused on the opening of the Coroner's Inquest. At 9:30 the Coroner's Jury gathered at the Court of Sessions to proceed with the first order of business, viewing the bodies of

the dead and wounded. Coroner Walters had provided five
carriages for James Perkins, the foreman, his fourteen jurymen, and Dr. Whitaker, the official medical examiner. Their
first stop was at the City Hospital, where, instead of finding
one deceased, as expected, they found two dead and one
dying.

The hospital's operating room had been a scene of great
activity that morning. Thomas Aylwood, whose thigh had
been fractured by a musket ball, was obliged to have his leg
amputated. He died immediately after the operation. Bridget
Fagan, who had been walking with her husband on the
night of the riot, two blocks away from the action, had,
according to the *Herald* (May 14), "received a musket ball
in the ham of the leg, the ball passing through fracturing
the end of the thigh bone and splintering the knee cap." Her
amputation was reported in minute, if varying, detail by all
the newspapers. The *Courier* (May 14) wrote that "the
patient was put under the influence of chloroform, and the
operation performed by Dr. J. Kearney Rodgers with his
usual ease, calmness and skill. We do not recall an amputation of the thigh in which so little blood was lost." On the
same day the *Herald* further noted that the "Doctors ad-
ministered ether, which lulled her off into a stupor, and
when she awoke she found herself in bed, doing well, minus
her leg; she was perfectly unconscious of having felt any
pain." Bridget was still alive when the jury paid its visit, but
she died the following Monday.

John Detzell had been put under the knife immediately
after Bridget Fagan. A shot in the groin had broken the
thigh bone "near the head." The wound was almost surely
mortal, but the surgeons offered the patient "the slight
chance afforded by amputation at the hip joint, the most
fearful operation in surgery. It was accepted by him and

performed by Dr. Rodgers." Detzell died right after the operation.

From the City Hospital the Coroner's carriages moved on to 472 Pearl Street. Here the body of Timothy Burns was examined. One juror reported that the "room was very close and warm, causing the body to be very offensive." The next stop was at 219 Sullivan Street. The Coroner knocked at the door, and, according to the *Daily Globe* (May 14),

A good looking young man came to appear and walked out on the stoop. The Coroner stated that he came to see the body of John S. Jones.

"Well," said the young man, "here I am."

"Yes," said the Coroner, laughing, "but I want to see the dead Jones."

"I am the only Jones here," answered Mr. Jones, "and, as for myself, I feel quite well. There was a young man brought here, slightly wounded, but he is doing quite well, and in no danger of dying."

This incident created quite a laugh. The jury took their seats again in the carriages, and drove to the Fifteenth Ward Station House.

The mission continued all morning, including a stop at 107 West Thirteenth Street, where the party descended to view the body of Timothy McGuire, a nineteen-year-old laborer and "the sole support of his aged mother." The Coroner was informed that "the body had been taken to Williamsburgh and interred, on a certificate given by Dr. Wagstaff. This will cause much trouble, as the body must be disinterred by the Coroner at Williamsburgh."

A little before two o'clock the entourage returned to the Tombs and decided to take a half-hour recess. As the *Herald* (May 13) explained it, ". . . their duties in the morning had been rather arduous, and as they had partaken of no refresh-

ment since morning, it was deemed expedient not to commence taking testimony on the inquest before half-past two
o'clock."

A large crowd had been on hand at the Halls of Justice
since early morning. They had waited patiently while the
jurors conducted their examining mission, not wishing to
give up the positions that they held in the courtroom. Others,
having been unable to squeeze into the building, were crowd-
ing the area in front.

When the session got under way, Mayor Woodhull and
General Sandford took seats near the Coroner. The scene
was reported in the same edition of the *Herald*:

> Woodhull looked tired and exhausted; he bore visible marks of
> mental anxiety and physical exertion which he underwent dur-
> ing the two days preceding. While giving his testimony, his voice
> was so low as to be inaudible at a distance of ten feet from where
> he sat. General Sandford, too, appeared to be much cast down,
> his face was sunburnt a great deal, and his voice was hoarse from
> a cold which he contracted in the discharge of his duties. During
> the taking of the testimony, notwithstanding, that the court room
> was filled, a dead silence prevailed; the falling of a pin even
> could be distinctly heard in any part. Every word which fell from
> the lips of the witnesses was eagerly caught; and in case anyone
> present imperfectly heard a particular sentence or a particular
> word, he immediately applied to the person next to him for a
> repetition of it.

The first witness was the Mayor. He detailed all of his
connections with the affair, beginning with the Thursday
afternoon meeting in his office and ending with his appearance at the Opera House that evening. General Sandford
followed with an account of his participation, giving full
information about all the military operations. At the conclu-

sion of Sandford's testimony, the Coroner adjourned the examination until ten o'clock Sunday morning.

The newspapers on Saturday not only gave full accounts of the meeting at the Park on Friday evening and the action at the Opera House, but began editorializing elaborately on all aspects of the affair. The opening paragraphs in the *Tribune* piece were typical.

Our city has been intensely agitated, a riot of a most outrageous and disgraceful character has taken place, the military have been called out, property destroyed, blood shed, and, for the last thirty-six hours, New York has worn the aspect of a civil war, all because two actors had quarrelled! The contrast between the fact and its consequences would make the whole seem absurd and incredible were not our streets even now lined with soldiers to prevent further outrage, while the stricken and sorrowing keep watch in desolate homes over the bodies of the dead.

Had none fallen in the affray but the real rioters who were personally engaged in the attack on the theatre and its legal defenders, however much the destruction of human life might be deplored, a certain justice in the event would strike every mind and strengthen the satisfaction natural to the lover of order, when Law triumphs over wanton and brutal violence. But on such an occasion the innocent and the guilty are struck down together, and however necessary the victory, there is something inexpressibly painful in its cost.

Some editors held that Macready should never have appeared, or that the performance should have been stopped at the first outbreak of violence. The *Herald* deplored the fact that such an outrage should have sprung from "a contemptible and paltry quarrel between two impudent, conceited play actors," and that it had been brought to the critical stage by the actions of the "silly committee" which petitioned Mac-

ready to go on. Some wondered if there had been sufficient
warning that the soldiers were going to fire. The *Express*
felt that the innocent spectators had really precipitated the
destruction. "It is the large number of lookers-on which
gives confidence to rioters by inducing them to suppose that
all by whom they are surrounded are engaged in the same
unlawful enterprise." The *Post,* although professing to have
"no clear convictions upon the whole subject," insisted that
the civil authorities must be upheld. "We should be the last
to utter one word of censure against its officers, and would
rather our right hand should burn, than that it would pen a
syllable calculated to weaken the moral effect of that dreadful discipline."

The *Express* printed a curious letter protesting their previous day's interpretation of the events:

To the Editors:

In your article, speaking of the late riot, you have seen proper
to make this remark concerning some of the wounded, "They
were youngsters, and seemed to be firemen." I would ask you,
as you state that you were on the spot, whether you are certain
they were firemen, or is your reporter in an underhanded manner, endeavoring to throw odium upon that department. I can
positively state that there were no firemen present excepting
those who were called out by the alarm at the time, and ex-
pecting that it had originated from the Opera House, immediately repaired to that place.

By inserting the above you will do justice to a body of men
who have unintentionally been slandered.

An Old Fireman.

(Editor: We are sure there was no intention to throw odium
upon Firemen,—and we know that Firemen's dress is often
assumed by mob rowdies, to disguise themselves.)

Although all the papers were agreed that "the peace and

good order of the city must be maintained at all hazards," only one, the *Tribune,* speculated on the lasting damage that might result from the riot. "The evils that follow such a conflict do not end with the repairing of the damages, nor even with the sorrow for the dead. They penetrate into all the relations of industry and of citizenship. They appear in the diminution of confidence in the silent and peaceful force of the law, in the weakening of neighborly feeling by those ferocious instincts which are alas! always but too strong and ready in every large city."

On Saturday evening, with the rumors still persisting that a "killer" force was on its way from Philadelphia, there was no disposition to slacken the military control over the Opera House area. The Mayor issued another proclamation from his office in the City Hall:

> The Mayor congratulates the citizens upon the spirit of obe-dience to the laws which, with few exceptions, pervaded the city last night, while he cannot too highly commend the alac-rity with which the Civil and Military force, as well as the great mass of the people, responded to the demand made by the au-thorities, in the name of the law, for the maintenance of public order.
>
> He trusts that a renewal of the disturbance of the past two nights is not to be apprehended; but at the same time he feels bound to urge upon the friends of order to abstain from fre-quenting the streets for a few nights to come.
>
> In the meantime, he assures the citizens that the whole civil and military force of the County continues actively engaged in the discharge of its duty, in upholding and maintaining, at every hazard, the peace of the city.
>
> CALEB S. WOODHULL, *Mayor.*

The Mayor's admonition, along with the rain that had been pouring down all day, put an effective dampener on any inclination that there might have been to renew the disturbance. When the military assumed their positions at seven o'clock Saturday evening, only a handful of spectators gathered around the Opera House. In fact the police managed to clear the entire area without any assistance from the soldiers.

Late in the afternoon the following division orders had been issued over the signatures of Major General Sandford and his Division Inspector, R. C. Wetmore:

FIRST DIVISION OF N. Y. S. MILITIA

May 12, 1849

The Major General expresses his thanks to the several corps ordered on duty on the 10th and 11th instant, for the prompt manner in which they assembled upon that notice, and their good order and discipline while under arms, and particularly to the seventh regiment, for their steadiness, firmness and forbearance under the most trying circumstances, on the night of the 10th inst.

The several corps detailed for duty by Special Orders, will be sustained by the whole division in case of emergency. The whole division will be assembled at the signal of seven strokes of the fire bells of the city, at their Regimental stations, where they will await the orders of the Major General.

The Major General deplores the necessity of enforcing the laws against our fellow citizens, but the peace of the city must be preserved.

In addition to this whole division of militia, the federal troops on Governor's Island and the Marine Corps at Brooklyn Navy Yard were also held in readiness. Called up by the special orders were the Seventh, Ninth, and Eleventh Regiments under Colonels Duryea, Borden, and Ferris. The troops took the same defense stations on Saturday night as on Friday night, and the "streets [were] enfiladed with cannon as they had been on the previous evening." Thus the barn door was not only locked but protected by artillery.

The reporters on the scene were hard put to it for any real news, though someone on the staff of the *Herald* (May 13) concocted a story out of "below-stairs" gossip:

Early in the evening, a number of solemn consultations were held among the domestics, white and colored, of Lafayette Place neighborhood. The discussion of the parlor and drawing room had found an echo in the kitchen and the pantry. While the respectable and comfortable occupants of those magnificent and elegantly furnished abodes of opulence and luxury were engaged in conversation about the occurrences of the week, the "domestics" also talked the matter over, expressed their opinions, and drew their own conclusions. On the whole, so far as we had an opportunity of judging, the good sense, the sound judgment, and the reverence for the great principles of justice, which characterized the deliberations of the kitchen, were at least fully equal to the councils of the drawing-room—for all were unanimous that they lived in trying times and a very dangerous neighborhood.

The only mild oubreak of the evening occurred about nine o'clock. Someone started a rumor that Macready had been shot in Boston. This, of course, spread like wildfire and brought cheers from the groups gathered in the Bowery, but there was no further attempt to raid the protectors of law and order.

Just after midnight, the streets being almost deserted, a portion of the military and all the police except those assigned to the Seventeenth District were dismissed. They marched together down Broadway. When they got in front of the New York Hotel, the rank and file moved on, but the officers turned into the Hotel "to partake of some refreshments." At three in the morning the remaining military forces were also discharged, the Seventeenth-District police being left in control.

Evidently most of the citizens of the city attended the Mayor's admonition to stay at home. Forrest played the last performance of his engagement that evening—appearing in his most popular vehicle, *Metamora*—but there was only a handful of people in the Broadway Theatre to give him a final cheer.

Thus the fatal week ended. The stars must have been in an unfavorable conjunction during this period, or, as the Philadelphia *Public Ledger* (May 21) put it, "Calamity treads upon the heels of calamity as though a sympathetic link connected disaster." During the unpropitious seven days, May 6 through May 12, the steamer *Empire* had gone down in the Hudson with nine drowned and ten missing. One fire had destroyed "half the flourishing business city of St. Louis," and another fire, in Watertown, Massachusetts, had burned out nearly a hundred buildings. New Orleans had also been afflicted, having suffered major property damage from a break in the levee.

On Sunday morning the Coroner's Inquest was resumed. Sheriff Westervelt gave his testimony and was followed by Chief of Police Matsell, Recorder Tallmadge, and Brigadier General Hall. Each related his own version of the riot, the details of which form the basis for the account already given. The witnesses were interrupted by an occasional question from a juror relative to the firing: "Who gave the order to fire?" "Was the crowd warned that they would be fired upon?" These the jurors regarded as the critical points. After Hall's testimony, the Coroner declared an hour's recess. When the jurymen reassembled, shortly after four, they heard the statements of some of the bystanders who had answered the Coroner's summons. Sylvester L. Wiley,

Stephen W. Gaines, Jesse Gilbert Haviland, and Thomas Velden, in that order, took the stand in the late afternoon session. By this time it was well past the dinner hour, and although some of the jurors favored sticking it out until midnight, Coroner Walters adjourned the Inquest after giving instructions that it would be continued the next day, Monday, May 14, at ten o'clock in the morning.

The Opera House was protected on Sunday evening just as it had been on the previous nights. Six hundred police were on duty, some occupying the building and the others disposed in a line encircling the entire area. No one was permitted inside the line without permission from Chief Matsell. The entire First Division of the State Militia was ordered to stand by, and the troops on Governor's Island and the Marines at the Brooklyn Navy Yard were again held in readiness. The Brigades of General Ewen and General Morris had been mustered in full force, numbering nearly seven hundred muskets. Ewen's forces were quartered at the University (Columbia), "where they were made as comfortable as circumstances would permit, and we take great pleasure in stating for the satisfaction of those accustomed to worship in the chapel there on Sundays, that we left the troops singing some of the most beautiful hymns we ever heard, thus affording a most gratifying evidence that the occasion which called them out, had not made them forgetful of the place in which they were posted, or the reverence due to the day." (This account appeared in the *Courier and Enquirer* for May 14.)

Morris' Brigade was stationed at the Arsenal. Early in the evening a messenger was sent from the Opera House to advise Morris that his troops would not be needed. Either the messenger was slow-footed or took a circuitous route; in either event, he missed Morris. The five hundred men with their battery of six-pounders reached the Washington Parade Ground before Morris received the order to dismiss his command.

The entire evening passed quietly at the Opera House. The continuing rain kept the would-be spectators indoors. At no time during the evening were more than fifty people gathered in the Bowery. The Mayor and a group of aldermen and members of the Common Council were on duty at the New York Hotel, but they were never obliged to deprive themselves of the comforts of that establishment. Earlier in the day the Mayor had feared that a disturbance might be precipitated by the "call" published in the *Herald* summoning two volunteer companies to appear on Monday night for "target practice." Even when he discovered that the announcement had not been authorized by any of the militia officers, he sent orders to Colonel Stewart not to pass out any arms unless they were officially requisitioned.

At ten o'clock Monday morning the Coroner's Jury was back in session. The jurors were not as well accommodated as they had been two days previously. Since the Court of Sessions was occupied with regular trials, the Coroner was obliged to move his inquisition to another part of the building. Sidney Stuart, Clerk of the Police, began the testimonies. When the critical questions about calling up the military and firing on the crowd were brought up, Stuart became evasive:

Coroner. From what you saw that evening previous to the firing of the Military, what is your opinion as to the capacity of the Civil Authority to disperse the mob, or the riot, without calling to their aid the Military?

Stuart. I don't choose to have it stated.

Coroner. It is a mere matter of opinion?

CLINTON HALL

Stuart. There are others more competent to give such an opinion.

Coroner. Is that the answer?

Stuart. No; only a remark.

After more badgering Stuart finally agreed that "The Police,
at the time of firing, could not have quelled the riot; for the
assault was entirely directed against the soldiers and not
against the house; that's all I desire to say on this part of
the subject."

Dennis Ryer, the former Police Captain, was the next
witness. He insisted that he had heard no "word given to the
crowd to disperse or they should be fired upon." He was
sure, too, that if the Chief of Police had exercised his authority, the mob could have been dispersed before the arrival of
the military.

The morning session concluded with the testimonies of
John Clark, a bookbinder, William McKinney, a policeman
of the Thirteenth Ward, and Bernard Manning. Manning
had not been at the scene. He merely wanted to make it
known that Thomas Kiernan was (as has been noted) "an
honest, sober, and steady man."

Shortly after two o'clock in the afternoon the jury reas-
sembled to hear the statements of John Lalor, Clerk of the
Third District Police; Captain Tilly, of the Thirteenth Ward
Police; Benjamin P. Fairchild, Captain of the Eighth Ward
Police; Henry Shumway, Captain of the Eighth Company
of the National Guards; John B. Levrich, a varnisher and
polisher; and Charles Cook, Assistant Police Captain of the
First Ward. The last testimony heard was that given by Dr.
John H. Whitaker, who provided a detailed description of
the injuries received by each of the deceased. The Coroner
then addressed the jury:

Gentlemen.—I believe with this testimony we will conclude. The testimony of Dr. Whitaker shows the nature and fatality of the wounds received by the deceased at the riot at the Astor Place Opera House. It is your duty now, gentlemen, to take into consideration the proceedings of Thursday—day and night—and the testimony adduced on the inquests, and if you find anything to censure or justify, taking the entire into consideration, let it come where it may, you should act fairly and independently.

At six-thirty the jurors retired, "officers being stationed at the doors to keep all persons from holding any conversation with them." After two and a half hours of deliberation, they returned to the courtroom with the verdict delivered and signed by James H. Perkins, Foreman:

We believe that George A. Curtis, John McDonald, *et al.* came to their deaths by gun shot wounds, fired by the military during the riot before the Opera House on Thursday evening 10th May instant, by order of the civil authorities of the city of New York, and that *the circumstances existing at the time* JUSTIFIED *the authorities in giving the order to fire upon the mob.* We further believe that if a larger number of the Police had been ordered out the necessity of a resort to the use of the military might have been avoided.

NEW YORK, May 14, 1849.

Thus the Inquest ended. The authorities had been officially vindicated—with reservations.

While the Coroner's Inquest was in session and even after the verdict had been given, the city remained quiet. There were some hints that the disturbance might break out again, but nothing came of them. An advertisement appeared in the papers urging all the members of the Empire Club to report for "target practice that evening," and a "conspicuous politician" received a letter from an importer of firearms advising him that he could be supplied with two thousand muskets and pistols with which to "oppose the authorities." (This turned out to be a "humbug" designed to embarrass the politician.) On Monday afternoon the funeral train of Peter Sampson, late member of the Washington Greys, passed through the city on its way to Greenwood Cemetery and "caused a great sensation." The rumor spread that Sampson had died from a fractured skull received in the melee of Thursday night. Actually, none of the military or police had been killed, and this intelligence fortunately became known before any damage was done.

On the same afternoon the Mayor held a meeting with his Board of Aldermen at which Alderman Kelly of the Sixth Ward presented a series of resolutions pertaining to the riot.

WHEREAS, The late lamentable occurrences which took place in our city on the night of the 10th instant, have cast a deep gloom over our whole citizens.

AND WHEREAS, It is due to this community, and to ourselves as representatives of the *people* of this city, to institute a thorough and searching examination into the merits of the case, and expose or explain how far those who, on behalf of the civil power, are blamable or justified in calling on an armed military force on the above-named night. Therefore,

Resolved, That a special committee of this Board be appointed to inquire into and investigate the late lamentable occurrences resulting in the destruction of so many valuable lives of our innocent fellow citizens, and whether or not the available civil force of this City was called out and so disposed of as to be able to protect the Astor Place Opera House without the intervention of a military force.

Resolved, That this Committee report as soon as practicable.

The resolutions were, however, immediately "laid upon the

table" to be brought up for reconsideration after the Coroner's report had been studied.

The Opera House neighborhood remained peaceful on Monday, and, since there seemed to be no further need for the military, Major General Sandford sent out the following orders to the First Division:

NEW YORK, May 14, 1849.

The Major General announces that the services of the Division (excepting the Corps ordered on special duty) are no longer deemed necessary by the magistrates upon the present occasion; but in the case of necessity, the whole division will assemble at their respective Regimental Stations upon the signal of seven strokes of the fire bells, and report forthwith to the Major General.

MAJ. GEN. SANDFORD
R. C. WETMORE, Division Inspector.

The police maintained their stations inside and outside the theatre throughout the day and night. A few spectators remained, but no more than the police could easily keep under control. The city was settling back to normal.

On Tuesday, the fifteenth, the interest of the city was focused on the funerals of the riot victims. No permission for interment could be given until the Coroner's Inquest had been completed. Now, with the hearings finished, the city became a scene of mass mourning. There were constant processions of black carriages during the entire afternoon. The mournful cavalcade accompanying Timothy Burns to his final resting in the graveyard of St. Patrick's Cathedral numbered some thirty vehicles. The various benevolent societies were out with their bands to usher their brothers to their last rest. The account in the *Herald* on the following day preserves the mood of the occasion.

The city yesterday, in almost every part, presented a scene of mourning, in consequence of the last tribute of respect to those who fell in the memorable and deplorable riot of Thursday night last. From almost every section passed a funeral train, composed of those who mourned the dead. Among those borne to their final resting places, were the innocent who imprudently, and through curiosity, attended the scenes of the fatal night; but they mingled in the crowd, and with the violator of the law fell, casting a melancholy and gloom around the once happy and cheerful fireside. That father who had sallied forth, mayhap to enjoy the pleasures of the evening, first imprinting upon the cheek of his prattling boy the kiss of affection, soon, by the fatal aim of the soldiers, ceased to be among the living. It is a melancholy thing, thus in one short hour to throw upon the young and happy wife the veil of widowhood, and upon those children buoyant with life, and with prospects of paternal guidance, the fate of the orphan. But they fell in the vindication of the law, and the preservation of the peace by the corporate authorities of the city. Many supposed that the appearance of those funeral trains would call forth the hidden vengeance of those who incited the riot on the occasion when they fell, and lead to further violations of the peace and quiet of the city; but all was still. Gloom had assumed the place of pleasure, and no disposition was manifested to wring the hearts of the grief-stricken, by the vicious and peace destroyers of the community. Never before was the city called upon to witness such a scene, and it is to be hoped, nay, it is hardly possible, that it ever will again. The day passed. The victims of the riot night slumbered in the tomb, and the city sank to reflection upon the melancholy duty which had been performed.

The funeral processions finally ended, without having provoked any disturbances, so the authorities decided to dismiss the police from the Opera House and return the building to the lessees, Messrs. Hackett and Niblo. Every day since the riot the managers had run a newspaper advertisement informing the public that the house had been closed by order of the civil authorities. On Thursday, May 17, the last of these advertisements appeared. Everyone now knew that the building would have to be closed for repairs and would have to await a new engagement.

The future did not look very bright for the Astor Place Opera House. Niblo's new theatre, on the site of his former Gardens, was to be ready for the opening performance on July 30. The *Herald* wrote on May 29, "As this theatre rises rapidly from the ground, the Opera House in Massacre Place—we mean Astor Place—sinks and fades. Indeed, the unfortunate and bloody events connected with that affair, coupled with its silly history for two or three years before, will lead to the necessity of closing it altogether as a place of public amusement. We would advise the proprietors of Massacre Place Opera House to convert it into a church— into a place for hearing sermons, and singing of psalms, and making prayers, and repenting of sin, for assuredly there has been enough of sin committed in that region to be repented of in sackcloth and ashes."

The proprietors would have been wise to follow this advice. The house opened again on September 24, 1849, for a brief period (lasting until October 8) of miscellaneous entertainment. Max Maretzek then had a disastrous season of opera, from November 1 to March 7 (1849–50). Not only were his audiences inadequate, but he was troubled with strikes among the musicians. During the rest of that spring there was an assortment of temporary tenants, and in the summer the Havana Opera Company tried a brief engagement, from June 3 to July 8. The season of 1850–51 was much the same. Maretzek engaged the house for still another season of opera (October 21 to March 27), but his audiences were drained away by Jenny Lind, who was then the rage of New York. The next season Maretzek tried

again, but with the same results. In June, 1852, the Opera
House was taken over by Donetti's Animal Troupe. Maretzek insisted that Niblo had connived at this move and that
he wanted to deal the theatre a final and fatal blow. Whatever the truth of these suspicions, the house never did recover
from the stigma of having served as a menagerie. On
August 30 Charles Thorne took over the establishment and
reopened it as the New York Theatre, hoping to improve
matters by changing the name; but after a short season of
such theatrical oddities as the Bateman sisters (Kate was
nine and Ellen seven) in the leading roles in *Richard III,*
the theatre was closed for good. The final performance was
that of a French troupe on October 20, 1852, in *La Grâce de
Dieu.*

On April 4, 1853, all the furnishings, properties, and scenery were put up for sale, and in 1854 the building was
purchased by the Mercantile Library Association and trans-
formed into the Clinton Hall Library. The purchase price
was $150,000, and an additional $115,000 were required for
remodeling. As the library was finally arranged, it had a first-
floor lecture room seating 1,000 and a second-floor reading
room which measured 60 by 90 feet. The 43,000 volumes
were kept in a large elliptically shaped room which occupied
two floors (the third and fourth) and was surrounded by
Corinthian columns and surmounted by a dome. The building also included a book-dealing service—conducted by the
Mercantile Library Association—which later became the
largest book market in the city; and half a block south, on
Lafayette Place opposite Astor's home, was the Astor Library, built in 1854 and housing a collection which, in 1895,
was consolidated with the other private libraries in the city to
form the main collection of the New York Public Library.
Today, of course, the neighborhood, particularly along

Fourth Avenue from Eighth Street to Fourteenth, is famous for its abundance of second-hand book stores.

The Opera House, though generally considered to have been designed for the taste, comfort, and edification of its patrons, seems to have been marked for failure almost from the date of its opening, in 1847. As a music and drama center, it lasted for only a little more than five years and was long outlived by its successor. Clinton Hall survived for thirty-six years, until April, 1890, when the building was vacated and torn down.

Hail to the Chief

★ ★ ★

Forrest closed his engagement at the Broadway on Saturday, May 12. He had made plans to take a week's rest and then reopen in Philadelphia on Monday, May 21; but before he left New York, he was taken ill and forced to cancel his Philadelphia engagement. If his illness came as an aftermath of the riot, no hint was given. His physician, Dr. John F. Gray, merely reported that "Forrest was severely indisposed."

Macready was at the home of George Ticknor Curtis in Boston waiting for the sailing of the *Hibernia*. Although the Mayor (of Boston) called to assure him that "every precaution would be taken by the authorities for his protection," Macready spent an uncomfortable twelve days. A group of his friends got up an elaborate statement pleading Macready's case. The statement was published in the Boston papers on the fifteenth and reprinted by the New York *Evening Post* the following day. This document, signed by Curtis, Prescott, and Hillard, among others, concluded with a properly genteel admonition: "Macready simply submitted himself to the wishes of his friends, as expressed in their letter, and to his own sense of the duty he owed to the citizens of New York; and in doing so, the public will judge whether he ought to carry away with him from this country any other feeling than that which every humane man must have when he finds his name in any way connected with so dreadful an occurrence, however innocent he may have been."

On the evening of May 20 Macready was given a farewell party by George Curtis. Curtis invited Longfellow, Dana, Judge and Mrs. Warren, David Colden, and a few other intimates; and Macready, touched by the loyalty of his friends, rewarded them with readings from Milton and Dryden.

The day before Macready's sailing, on Tuesday, May 22, the New York *Morning Express* reported that "Mr. Macready has transmitted from Boston to Mayor Woodhull, of this city, $1,000 to be given to necessitous relatives of the persons killed in the recent riot at the Opera House." Macready later denied this. While he was in Boston, his only thought was to be out of the country as quickly as possible and to forget the riot. He finally departed on the morning of May 23. He and Curtis went by carriage and ferry to East Boston, where Macready boarded the *Hibernia*. "I never felt such relief," he wrote later, "as in planting my foot on that vessel's deck."

By this time, however, the possibility of additional violence had been pretty well dissipated. The Opera House was closed for repairs, Forrest was still confined to his bed, many of the rioters were still in jail awaiting trial, and those who were free were indisposed to further hostility. Repercussions were still being felt, but these were entirely journalistic. The events and the entire background of the riot were endlessly reviewed by the press, often in a mood of extreme partisanship, and accusations were freely expressed.

The *Journal of Commerce* (May 17) held that the signers of the petitioning letter to Macready were "mainly instrumental in bringing this calamity on our city." The house should have been closed. "Is it not the Christian's duty to give no cause for offense, but rather 'to remove the stumbling block from a brother's path?'" The *Tribune* (May 18) asked the correspondent of the *Journal of Commerce* "to review calmly the opinion so hastily expressed. . . . If a newspaper editor can express his opinions in his columns, may not individual citizens express theirs in a letter?"

The *Courier and Enquirer* (May 14) held that if the proprietors of the Opera House had been obliged to close their doors, a fateful blunder would have been committed. This "would have placed the mob above the law, and have cost thereafter ten times the number of lives now sacrificed to have re-established the majesty of the laws. . . ." The *Journal of Commerce* (May 21) had exactly the opposite opinion: "The actor's rights are unlike the natural rights of man or citizens; the former are permitted, the latter must be protected; the former may properly be suspended when necessary for the public peace, while the latter must for public good be maintained even against the threats of mobs."

The *Evening Post* (May 16) in a full-column piece entitled "Whose Is the Fault?" insisted that neither the Macready supporters nor the authorities who permitted the Opera House to remain open should be blamed and then went on to uphold the rights of minorities to the full protection of the law. According to the *Post*, this "doctrine" of minority rights was quite "as applicable to the case of a theatrical performance as it is to the case of a public meeting for other purposes."

In the majority opinion of the press neither the signers of the letter nor the authorities could be charged with any crime in encouraging or permitting Macready to proceed with his performance. It can be safely conjectured, however, since the newspapers devoted so much space to making this point, that the opposite position was widely held among the public.

The Philadelphia press, as has been noted, charged that the New York newspapers were in a large measure responsible for precipitating the riot. The *Public Ledger* wrote on May 14, "Not a journal, no, not one! appealed to the good sense, love of order, respect for public and private right and personal dignity, of partisans on either side." Rather surprisingly, a New York paper concurred in this opinion. On May 15 the *Tribune* concluded its riot editorial with the following paragraph:

But the most direct agency of disorder is yet to be spoken of. We mean the licentious, unprincipled and venal press—the press which sells its influence to the most corrupt uses, which sneers at benevolence and mocks at religion, which has neither faith in men, reverence for God, nor belief in anything, which panders to depraved appetites, traffics in falsehood and calumny, speculates on dishonor; gloats over vice, and does its utmost to weaken the moral sense of the public and bring the law into contempt. Who will estimate the part which this branch of the newspaper press has had in bringing about the Astor Place riot? Who can tell how much of the violence there displayed was the fruit of its insidious assaults on all that is best and most sacred? And by whom is such a press kept in existence? That, too, reader, is a question which we leave for you to reflect on.

The out-of-town newspapers editorialized at length about the riot. The general drift of comment and interpretation proceeded along the lines taken by the local press, but a few observations are typical enough or lively enough to be included here and will serve to indicate that the troubles in Astor Place excited pretty general interest. With the exception of the Boston *Traveller* (May 17) the quotations from U.S. papers outside New York were all dated May 16.

The Baltimore *Sun* considered the whole affair "a melancholy exhibition of popular frailty, and a sure indication that there are principles yet to be taught and practices yet to be learned." The Washington *National Era* felt that there had been too much sympathy for the rioters. The Boston *Traveller* regretted that "respectable men [the signers of the letter to Macready] and newspaper editors have seen fit to dignify the paltry quarrel of two actors." The Rochester *American* insisted that "the laws must be maintained at all hazards, violence will sometimes submit to nothing but force." The *North American* and the *Times and Keystone,* both Philadelphia papers, had similar opinions. On the technical question of musket fire *versus* mobs, the Boston *Times* thought that "the only fault was in using blank cartridges at the first firing, or rather firing over the heads of the mob. Napoleon's rule is the right one in such cases; fire with ball first and then use only powder."

The municipal authorities were also censured. The Philadelphia *Pennsylvanian* felt that "there was no provocation for such a fatal interposition," and the Albany *Atlas* found an "infinite disproportion between the retaliation and the provocation. It was the duty of the magistracy to act with intelligence, with humanity, and even with mercy. . . ."

Much additional space was, of course, devoted to the two principals. The Philadelphia *Bulletin* was "exasperated to think that two strolling actors—talented indeed, but still only strolling actors—should have the power, the one by playing on national prejudices, the other by invoking the national honor, to plunge a great city into riot and blood. . . . If Union Square [now, of course, a downtown commercial area] chose to cry up Macready, it was no reason why the Bowery should cry him down." The Newburyport *Herald* put the blame on Forrest, "the man who by his ungentlemanly conduct, and ill temper, prepared the way for these outrages. Against Forrest, himself, does this bloody scene cry most loudly." The Albany *Knickerbocker* shared this view, but the Philadelphia *Sun* was "among those who despise Mr. Macready, with an earnestness of contempt which language cannot express; we believe him to be cravenhearted, egotistical, cold, selfish, inflated—a mere machine as an actor, and no more entitled to be called a genius than the organ pipes which thunder out the diapason. . . ."

In Canada the Quebec *Chronicle* (May 14) found in the occasion an excuse for criticizing the New York press. This criticism was expressed in a spirit of *quid pro quo,* some of the New York papers having previously commented on the vandalism which led to the destruction (already alluded to) of the Parliamentary library in Montreal. The Montreal *Courier* (May 16) advised the Canadian authorities to take a lesson from the Opera House riot and complained, apropos of the disastrous experience of the "volunteer cavalry troops employed in New York," that "too much money has been wasted on the Mounted Police."

The newspapers, both local and out of town, continued

until the end of May to exert themselves in behalf of their various views on and theories about the riot. Mob violence was widely and more or less uniformly deplored, but there was little agreement about the means of dealing with it. The decisions and actions of the magistrates (the Mayor, the Chief of Police, the Recorder, *et al.*) were sometimes praised and sometimes condemned. There were occasional lectures on tactics and numerous opinions about the cowardice, courage, resourcefulness, and ineffectiveness of the police and the militia.

The class-conflict implications were also lengthily expounded upon. The *Home Journal,* which later became *Town and Country,* picked up this theme in an article that appeared on May 12. ". . . the 'White and Red Roses of York and Lancaster' were never more distinctly divided into antagonistic parties, than the 'B'hoys' of New York and the 'Upper Ten.' . . . Let but the more passive aristocratic party clearly select a favorite, however, and let there be but a symptom of a handle for the 'B'hoys' to express their dissent, and the undercurrent breaks forth like an uncapped hydrant. . . . The white handkerchiefs that waved all over the boxes and parterre diffused an atmosphere that made the house as fragrant as a perfumer's shop; while the rotten eggs, potatoes, pennies and coarse placards equally betrayed the domestic habits of the opposition. . . . Macready's real offence, in the eyes of those who drove him from the stage, is in being rather rancidly superfine in his personal manners, and in being dined out continually by the uptowners."

On May 14 the New York correspondent of the Philadelphia *Public Ledger* reported: "There is a bitterness and a rancor remaining behind, which I fear will manifest themselves on future occasions. It leaves behind a feeling to which this community has hitherto been a stranger . . . a feeling that there is now in our country, in New York City, what every good patriot hitherto has considered it his duty to deny—a *high* and a *low* class." Subsequent editorials in the *Ledger* exonerated "the poor" from any responsibility for the social unrest that was found to exist and sternly concluded that "the aristocracy of our republican country" consisted of those "who assume exclusive privileges [and] exercise them through fraud or assert them by force." According to the *Tribune* (May 15), the cities, with their large populations of poor people, immigrants, and adventurers, were natural centers of mob violence. "Is there no means," the editor asked, "of preventing so many young men from rushing to the cities, of giving the less fortunate, the poor, a direct personal interest in the property and order of society, so that when it is attacked they shall feel that they are themselves attacked?" On the following day the *Herald* went to work on the "anarchical and destructive doctrines" disseminated by the *Tribune,* that "organ of French socialism and kindred abominations," and wondered how much mischief "may have been wrought amongst ourselves, by this continual harping upon the tyranny and oppression of the rich...."

It is hardly necessary to add that journalists in 1849 were not students of propaganda analysis. Nevertheless, they may have intuited something of the underlying significance of what had happened. Nearly three quarters of a century later Walter Lippmann wrote: "In the great blooming, buzzing confusion of the outer world we pick out what our culture has already defined for us, and we tend to perceive that which we have picked out in the form stereotyped for us by our culture." The stereotypes of the Astor Place riot were, of course, Forrest and Macready—Forrest, the brave, forthright, true-blue son of America, and Macready, the haughty, overbearing, aristocratic Britisher. Stereotypes, as Lippmann has pointed out, are likely to have some foundation in truth, but their function is precisely that of simplifying it or suppressing it. Becoming sharpened and clarified through use and receiving social approval, they eliminate the pain of reflection and judgment and sometimes, as in the riot in Astor Place, serve as mechanisms of rage and violence.

In the minds of the rioters, Forrest and Macready were, to use another of Lippmann's phrases, "constructed personalities." Tiresome and rather unsensational truths had yielded to, or been assimilated into, symbols which proved to be wonderfully effective in the mobilizing of opinions and emotions. The lines were clearly drawn between the "common man" (who was also, by some weird association of mob reasoning, a kind of latter-day Revolutionary War hero) and the hateful and easily hated caricature of British tyranny and oppression.

The trial of the rioters was considerably less glamorous than the Bowery B'hoys, in their excess of superheated patriotism, might have wished. Ten of the rioters—the others had been released for want of evidence—were brought before Judge Daly in the Court of General Sessions. The proceedings began on Wednesday, September 12, but it took until the following Monday to impanel an acceptable jury. The jury which was finally sworn in consisted of a liquor dealer, a tinsmith, a public-house keeper, a dry-goods merchant, a fruit merchant, and seven grocers.

The trial opened with Judge Daly's charge to the jury—a full hour of platitudinous oratory in which he said in part:

It is seldom, gentlemen, that a jury of this country is called to the discharge of a duty so grave and important as that which will be brought before you in connection with this deplorable occurrence. . . . If there is a government, gentlemen, upon earth, in which an unauthorized resort to violence is entirely without excuse, it is that under which we live. In other countries, where the modern political maxim prevails, of everything for the people, but nothing by them—where government is a thing apart, and the great majority of the governed have no voice in the regulation of the institutions by which they are ruled—it is not surprising that they should occasionally resort to violence to obtain their rights, no other remedy being left to them. But under institutions like ours, where every man is an integral part of the government, and has a voice in the creation of its laws; where the remedy for redressing grievances and reforming abuses is both certain and speedy, an unauthorized appeal to physical force is wholly without apology. Obedience to the laws of his own creation is the first duty of the citizen, and when he refuses to render it, he contravenes the great principle which holds a republican community together.

Judge Daly then proceeded with an extended exposition of the necessity for preserving the supremacy of the law. The gist of this statement is quoted here: "It is only by maintaining the laws, that the liberty of the individual can be protected. It is the only safeguard to secure it from popular violence or aristocratic encroachment."

Specifically, the jury had to determine whether or not there were evidence of conspiracy and/or riot. "Any combination of two or more persons to commit an offence is a conspiracy. . . . Any tumultuous assemblage of three or more persons brought together for no legal or constitutional object, deporting themselves in such manner as to endanger the public peace and excite terror and alarm in rational and firm-minded persons, is unlawful; and whenever three or more persons, in a tumultuous manner, use force or violence in the execution of any design wherein the law does not allow the use of force, they are guilty of a riot." The jury was not to concern itself with the degree of guilt. "All who have participated are to be jointly indicted, and jointly tried. The

only discrimination which the law makes, is the discretion
given to the court in apportioning the degree of punishment."

The first four days were devoted to the case for the prose-
cution, and the next three to the evidence for the defense.
On the whole the trial seems to have been a pretty tedious
affair. The defense, consisting of ten lawyers (one for each
prisoner), presented scores of witnesses who had been inti-
mate with the prisoners from childhood and many employers
who testified to the good characters of the accused, arousing
a good deal of sympathy for "the unfortunate young boys."
On Tuesday, the twenty-fifth, the defense counsel began
their summing up. Their pleas were the only high points in
the entire proceedings. On the twenty-sixth, the New York
Tribune reported, "Mr. Blankman, counsel for the defend-
ant Bennett, made an able appeal. Mr. Sherwood, counsel
for Matthews, followed in a speech of much sense and ability.
Then came Mr. Boudnito, counsel for Hossack; Mr. Cornell
in a touching speech for Adriance, and Mr. Busteed, Jr., in
a straightforward defense of Douglas." These final arguments went on for the remainder of the week.

All ten of the prisoners were found guilty and sentenced
to prison terms ranging from one month to one year. E. Z. C.
Judson ("Ned Buntline") was given the maximum that the
law permitted, one year in jail and a fine of $250. The others
had the sympathy of the court. "They were fearfully guilty,
but ignorant, excited, and misled"—nothing was to be gained
by vindictiveness. They had been judged guilty, and thus the
supremacy of law and order had been affirmed. That was
enough. As the *Tribune* wrote on October 6, "If guilty participation was not brought home to the arraigned, then it
would be idle to hope to do it in any case, and proclamation
might as well be made that any assemblage of boys and

men might tear down anybody's house on any dark night with impunity, though resisted by the police and watched by hundreds of people. . . . What society needs is prevention for the future, not vengeance for the past."

Any further assessment of guilt and responsibility would be superfluous and misleading. With all the intriguing items of evidence and pages of testimony that were available to them, one can easily enough understand why some reporters, at the time of the riot and later, chose to blame Forrest's hiss (and his equally blameworthy temper) or Macready's conceit and arrogance or the itching belligerence of the Bowery B'hoys or the decisions and actions of the Magistrates; but it would be grossly unfair to assign the ultimate responsibility to Forrest or Macready and considerably at odds with the facts to pinpoint any single incident as the one that triggered the outbreak of violence. About all that can be (briefly) said is that the riot arose from the peculiar combination of circumstances and personalities that existed in New York during the week of May 7, 1849, and even this statement, which leaves out of consideration all the antecedent misunderstanding and hostility, is incomplete.

The paths of Macready and Forrest never crossed again. Each was too occupied with his own affairs to have any thought for the other. Macready continued to perform in London and the provinces, but he was still tormented by unenthusiastic audiences, incompetent actors, and an unappreciative press. The lingering illness of his favorite child, Christine, who died on February 24, 1850, obsessed his mind, and after her death, he became even more bitter about continuing to perform in a theatre unworthy of his talents. On February 26, 1851, he gave his final farewell, a performance of *Macbeth* at Drury Lane. His remaining years—he died on April 27, 1873—were spent in retirement.

NED BUNTLINE
(Elmo Z.C. Judson)
Author of "SCOUTS OF THE PRAIRIE"

Forrest continued to be burdened with his quarrel with Catherine Sinclair. Before the divorce trial, with its charges of infidelity on both sides, Forrest and his wife had kept up a steady stream of acrimonious correspondence. The trial was begun on December 18, 1851, and lasted until January 24, 1852. The court awarded Mrs. Sinclair, as she then chose to call herself, $3,000 alimony per year and vindicated her of all charges. Forrest never accepted this judgment and continued to take his case to the people at every opportunity. On February 9, 1852, when he began an engagement at the Broadway, he was greeted with thundering applause and a banner hoisted by Captain Rynders reading, "This is the People's Verdict." Forrest appeared before the curtain, recognizing the intent of the applause, and spoke: "Ladies and gentlemen, I submit my cause to you,—my cause, did I say?—no, not my cause alone, but yours, the cause of every man in the community, the cause of every human being, the cause of every honest wife, the cause of every virtuous woman, the cause of everyone who cherishes a home and the pure spirit which should abide there. I submit my cause to a tribunal uncorrupt and incorruptible; I submit it to the sober second thought of the people. A little while since I thought my pathway was filled with thorns; you have this night filled it with roses."

Forrest's violent temper was not to be quieted by court action or roses. After reading an article by N. P. Willis condemning his conduct, he met Willis on Fifth Avenue, just below Fourteenth Street, and horsewhipped him. For this Forrest was obliged to pay $2,500 damages and court costs. But with all these personal troubles, his theatrical tours ranged wider and longer, and his box-office receipts reached an all-time high. In 1861–62, he made a hundred-night tour of the country; and in 1871–72, he travelled seven thousand

miles playing in fifty-two different cities. In Chicago—this
was January, 1866—his personal take was $11,600 for five
nights. He was undisputedly *the* American actor. The "Easy
Chair" (*Harper's Monthly Magazine,* December, 1862) was
shocked at meeting a man who had never seen Forrest. "If
he had said that he had never seen Trinity Church, or the
Astor House, it would have been strange; but to aver that he
had never seen Forrest was to tax credibility."

The tour of 1871–72 was Forrest's last. In the fall season of
1872, his rheumatism and gout kept him close to home and
limited his performances to some public readings. The last of
these was a reading of *Othello* at the Tremont Temple in
Boston on December 7, 1872. He died in Philadelphia five
days later.

It was one of the supporting players, rather than either of
the two principals, who acted out the final episode of the
riot. When Buntline, the rowdies' ringleader, was released
from his year's incarceration on Blackwells Island, his friends
escorted him from the prison in an open barouche drawn by
six white horses and accompanied by a brass band playing
"Hail to the Chief."

Sources and References

THE FOLLOWING information is supplied for those readers who may wish to acquaint themselves further with the background of the Astor Place riot or with the careers of Forrest and Macready. Some additional sources are cited in the notes to the text, pages 239–43.

The story of the riot itself was largely developed from accounts in New York and out-of-town newspapers, all dating from 1849:

NEW YORK

Daily Globe, Evening Post, Herald, Journal of Commerce, Morning Courier and Enquirer, Morning Express, Tribune

OUT OF TOWN

Philadelphia Public Ledger, Washington National Era, Washington Daily National Intelligencer

A few brief passages from the foregoing have been introduced into the text without specific identification.

Only one small pamphlet, the *Account of the Terrific and
Fatal Riot at the Astor Place Opera House,* by R. H. Ranney
(New York, 1849), has dealt exclusively with the riot. Other
articles and books include short sections on it and supply
additional detail on earlier riots in Great Britain:

"Famous Theatrical Riots," *Chamber's Journal of Popular
    Literature, Science, and Arts,* LXV (April 7, 1888), 222–24.
Headley, Joel Tyler. *The Great Riots of New York, 1712–
    1873.* New York, 1873.
Williams, Noel. "Some Famous Theatrical Riots," *Argosy,*
    LXXII (Oct., 1900), 224–29.

BOOKS ABOUT FORREST

Alger, William R. *Life of Edwin Forrest.* 2 vols. Philadel-
    phia, 1877.
Barrett, Lawrence. *Edwin Forrest.* Boston, 1881.
Harrison, Gabriel. *Edwin Forrest.* Brooklyn, 1889.
Moses, Montrose. *The Fabulous Forrest.* Boston, 1929.
Rees, James. *The Life of Edwin Forrest.* Philadelphia, 1874.

BOOKS ABOUT MACREADY

Archer, William. *William Charles Macready.* New York,
    1890.
Pollock, Sir Frederick, ed. *Macready's Reminiscences and
    Selections from his Diaries and Letters.* New York, 1875.
Toynbee, William, ed. *The Diaries of William Charles Mac-
    ready.* 2 vols. New York, 1912.
Trewin, J. C. *Mr. Macready.* London, 1955.

THEATRE HISTORIES

Hornblow, Arthur. *A History of the Theatre in America from its Beginning to the Present Time.* 2 vols. Philadelphia, 1919.

Ireland, Joseph N. *Records of the New York Stage from 1750 to 1860.* 2 vols. New York, 1866.

Moody, Richard. *America Takes the Stage.* Bloomington, Ind., 1955.

Nicoll, Allardyce. *History of Early Nineteenth Century Drama 1800–1850.* Cambridge, Eng., 1930.

———. *History of Late Nineteenth Century Drama 1850–1900.* Cambridge, Eng., 1947.

———. *The English Theatre.* New York, 1936.

Odell, George C. D. *Annals of the New York Stage.* 15 vols. New York, 1927–49. Volumes III, IV, and V cover the period from 1821 to 1850.

Quinn, Arthur Hobson. *History of the American Drama from the Beginning to the Civil War.* New York, 1923 and 1943.

———. *History of the American Drama from the Civil War to the Present Day.* New York, 1927 and 1943.

Rowell, George. *The Victorian Theatre.* London, 1956.

Watson, Ernest Bradlee. *Sheridan to Robertson.* Cambridge, Mass., 1926.

CHAPTER I

Macready's account of the events is from his *Diaries,* ed. William Toynbee, 2 vols. (New York, 1912).

CHAPTER II

Kemble's part in the O. P. riots is well reported in Herschel Baker, *John Philip Kemble* (Cambridge, Mass., 1942).

CHAPTER III

Pages 29–30

Whitman's report on the Bowery audience is from his "The Old Bowery," in *November Boughs* (Philadelphia, 1888), p. 90.

Page 32

The episode on board the American warship at Genoa is from Moses, *The Fabulous Forrest* (Boston, 1929), p. 124.

Pages 32–33

The Letter regarding King Louis Phillippe is quoted by Alger, *Life of Edwin Forrest* (Philadelphia, 1877), I, 269.

Page 33

Forrest's curtain speech is quoted by Moses, p. 136.

Page 40

Catherine's first impression of Forrest is quoted by Alger, I, 321.

CHAPTER IV

Page 43

The entire address by Forrest was printed under the title, *Oration Delivered at the Democratic Republican Celebration of the Sixty-Second Anniversary of the Independence of the United States in the City of New York, Fourth July, 1838* (New York, 1838).

Page 45

Ludlow devotes an extended passage to Macready in his *Dramatic Life as I Found it* (St. Louis, 1880), pp. 591–97.

Page 46

Mrs. Macready's letter to Forrest is quoted by Moses, p. 204.

Pages 48–49

Mitchell's and Bulwer-Lytton's letters are from *The Replies from England to Certain Statements Circulated in This Country Respecting Mr. Macready* (New York, 1849).

Page 55

John Coleman's account of Macready's Hamlet is from his *Fifty Years of an Actor's Life* (New York, 1904), II, 343–44.

CHAPTER V

Page 62

Forrest's curtain speech is quoted by Moses, pp. 228–39.

Page 64

Mrs. Drew's comment on Macready is from her *Autobiographical Sketch* (New York, 1899), p. 95.

Pages 64–65

George Vandenhoff's description of Macready is from his *Leaves from an Actor's Notebook* (New York, 1860), pp. 222–23.

Page 66

Dickens' letter is quoted in Macready's *Diaries,* Sept. 6, 1848.

Pages 77–78

Macready's card is from *The Replies from England.*

CHAPTER VI

Page 83

The Jamieson episode is described by Rees, *Life of Edwin Forrest,* p. 355.

Page 84

The speech at the Fonthill roofing ceremony is quoted by Moses, p. 273.

Page 84

Forrest's letter from Baltimore is quoted by Moses, p. 270.

Page 85

Lawson's letter to Sinclair is quoted by Moses, p. 277.

CHAPTER VIII

The accounts of the riot given by the officials and other witnesses are taken from testimony recorded at the Coroner's Inquest as reported in the *Evening Post, Herald, Daily Globe,* and *Tribune* on May 14 and 15, 1849.

Pages 130–32

The report on Buntline is from Jay Monaghan, *The Great Rascal, Life and Adventures of Ned Buntline* (Boston, 1952), p. 174. Additional information regarding Buntline can be found in Fred F. Pond, *Life and Adventures of Ned Buntline* (New York, 1919).

CHAPTER IX

Pages 180–81

Hone is quoted from *The Diary of Philip Hone,* edited by Allan Nevins (New York, 1927), I, 866–67.

Pages 198–99

Strong's comments were found in *George Templeton Strong's Diary,* edited by Allan Nevins and Milton Halsey Thomas (New York, 1952), I, 351–53.

CHAPTER X

The testimony of witnesses at the Inquest is as reported in the *Evening Post* for May 14 and 15, supplemented by the *Daily Globe, Herald,* and *Tribune* of the same dates.

CHAPTER XI

Page 229

The Lippmann quote is from his *Public Opinion* (New York, 1922) p. 81.

Pages 230–31

Judge Daly's charge is cited from *The Western Law Journal,* 7 (New series, Vol. 2, no. 2—Nov., 1849), 68–75.

Page 235

Forrest's speech is quoted by Moses, p. 296.

In addition to the sources of information included above, I have drawn on the material and professional resources of Indiana University. Specifically, I wish to acknowledge the aid given me by the Graduate School and to thank Walter Albee, of the Indiana University Press, for his patient and able assistance in editing and designing this book.

Date Due

JAN 2 1 1987		
JAN 3 0 1998		

Demco 293-5